T0115092

Karate for Kids
and for
Mom and Dad, Too

Vincent A. Cruz

Illustrated by Edward Luena

iUniverse, Inc.
Bloomington

Karate for Kids and Mom and Dad, Too

iUniverse books may be ordered through booksellers or by contacting:

iUniverse
1663 Liberty Drive
Bloomington, IN 47403
www.iuniverse.com
1-800-Authors (1-800-288-4677)

ISBN: 978-1-4759-5881-2 (sc)
ISBN: 978-1-4759-5883-6 (hc)
ISBN: 978-1-4759-5882-9 (e)

Printed in the United States of America

iUniverse rev. date: 02/08/2013

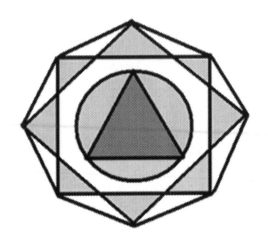

三天空手道協会

Endorsed by the
International San Ten Karate Do Association

Contents

Foreword

Occasionally, upon personal reflection, we reach a level of awareness where we are able to recognize the significance and effect others have on our development as spiritual beings. These rare and special people touch us with their wisdom and provide insight into life's many mysteries. From the lessons they provide, we uncover the ability to question our own actions and, in doing so, discover the means to initiate positive change for ourselves. As we acknowledge our blessings, we realize the need—no, the appropriateness—of expressing our gratitude for all we have gained.

I met Vincent Cruz almost by accident. I had trained in Shotokan karate for a number of years and was already a black belt at the time. I was training hard and with great dedication; however, I felt that something was missing. A freak skiing accident resulted in my leg being broken into ten spiral pieces. For nine months, I was non-weight bearing on the affected leg, and it was close to a year before I could start light karate training. Today, I have nineteen screws and three titanium plates as a permanent reminder of the event. The good (if that is possible) to come out of this event was the unlikely chance I met Master Cruz, a man who would come to be my teacher, and more importantly, my friend.

All who engage in martial arts understand that the relationship between student and sensei is one of reverence and dedication. Words cannot adequately express the mutual respect for one another that develops along their respective journeys of enlightenment. I have been very fortunate to be a direct student of Master Vincent Cruz, for whom I presently have the honor of serving as his sempai. During the time spent with Master Cruz, in training as well as personal interaction, I have had the rare opportunity to share many of his thoughts about the teaching and practice of traditional karate. One of those thoughts pertains to the teaching of karate for children.

In writing *Karate for Kids*, Cruz has cleverly addressed several important areas of need. Karate is a growing phenomenon in the

United States and internationally, and adults as well as children of all ages have discovered this exciting Japanese martial art. A great variety of works have appeared on the art of karate; nevertheless, there remains confusion and considerable discussion on the topic involving the distinction and differences between traditional Japanese karate and sport karate. Additionally, most literature that addresses karate presents in a fashion not easily understood by children and young practitioners. Few publications or books have been written with the intent or purpose of filling this void. In *Karate for Kids,* Cruz carefully crafts a book that presents the essential physical and philosophical elements of karate. His masterpiece makes for easy reading and is equally understandable for all ages. Its goal is to provide clear and purposeful instruction for the young practitioner in a way that reinforces and facilitates regular dojo training and thereby enhances the martial arts experience.

Karate, as we know it, is only a couple of hundred years old. It developed on the Ryukyu Islands, the largest of which is Okinawa. Its roots are immersed in the various Chinese styles, which were passed on to Okinawa as a result of trade between the kingdoms over the centuries and eventually fused with the numerous family "ryus" already in existence. In the early days, its purpose was for self-defense and personal preservation. It was a matter of life and death, and there were no rules. No sense of sport existed, and its ultimate purpose was clear. With the passage of time and modernization of most eastern civilizations, the need for such drastic application waned, and the focus and intent of training shifted. No longer was the study of karate performed with the urgency fostered by medieval life; its focus shifted to conditioning and competition. This has led to the development of what we refer to as "sports karate," in which rules regulate and control the application of technique by the competitors.

After World War II, karate's worth for self-defense, physical fitness, competition, and overall mental and physical development came to be more and more recognized worldwide. As a martial art, however, it necessitated long and carefully repeated study. Along with its growth and popularity, the seemingly grueling requirements of its study came to be overridden by the demands of today's world for more rapid results and quicker development. The result was the emergence of many new sports using the name of karate. To avoid confusion with these new sports, longtime practitioners began distinguishing the original karate as "traditional karate."

The teachings of traditional karate, through Master Cruz, are focused on and intended to stress the foundational principles on which traditional karate was created. In *Karate for Kids*, those principles are made available to young karateka in a format that is directly intended for their comprehension and ultimately enhances their personal development in this wonderful martial art. As it is an honor to be associated with Master Cruz, it is likewise an honor to now introduce to all *Karate for Kids*.

Steven W. P. Oliver, Renshi, Sixth Dan

Preface

Many books and manuals have been published with different styles and systems of Japanese, Korean, and Chinese martial arts. I have also found a few books for our youth. However, these books have been selective in the different styles of sports karate. Since there was virtually nothing available in traditional karate other than Master Hidetaka Nishiyama's text *Karate: The Art of Empty-Hand Fighting* and the comprehensive *The Textbook of Modern Karate* by Teruyuki Okazaki[1], I thought it would be proper at this time to write a young people's book on the traditional system of karate as expressed by the late Grandmaster Hidetaka Nishiyama.

For many years, my beginning students, young and old alike, have expressed a growing interest in having available a karate book covering specific instruction in learning and practicing individual techniques. Since karate instruction is immeasurable, I considered how to best undertake this exhausting task. There have been many excellent books published on karate; however, I find them filled with unnecessary material and too advanced for this stage of development.

What I have tried to present in this book is an introduction to traditional karate as an exciting healthful physical art and an effective form of self-defense. I have covered all three of its main aspects: (1) physical, (2) mental, and (3) spiritual. If this first book helps the reader to understand and perform better, then my efforts will have been rewarded. There will probably be many words you don't understand at first, and I have included a Glossary at the end to help you with their meanings.

I have dedicated this work to those young students who have stuck it out judiciously practicing the karate discipline. I wish there were more of them. I often see young people who do not know or care what to do with their free time. They move from one distraction

---

1 Teruyuki Okazaki, member of the Japanese Karate Association and student of Gichin Funakoshi.

to another and often end up in failure and full of boredom. The point that strikes me is these young people don't want to do anything on their own—they want to be entertained. One looks at their empty faces in amusement arcades spending their allowances on things with no return. Their leisure lacks goals, and they move about in aimless wandering. Joy lies in a seemingly pointless belief, and human values so treasured in the past are diminished. Without meaningful goals, their futures are in question. I would like to believe that these young people can develop a sense of worth through traditional karate. Karate stands as a philosophy that can help youth to master life with an inner respectability.

Hanshi Vincent A. Cruz

Acknowledgments

The following acknowledgments are not intended to imply, directly or indirectly, any endorsement of this work or to relieve the author of his full responsibility thereof.

The invaluable assistance rendered by my friend and artist, Edward Luena, has been a blessing. His illustrations make the text come alive, and without his tireless efforts, this story would not be complete.

Sensei Steven Oliver, who assisted me with this manuscript, has spent countless hours at my side with his guidance, suggestions, and support of my endeavors.

Kyoshi Bruce Clayton, who saw the manuscript and illustrations through the final steps to publication.

I am eternally grateful to these men for taking the time from their busy schedules to share in my dream.

Chapter One — What Is Karate?

Why do people practice karate? Where did it come from?

Modern Karate

Karate means *empty hand* in Japanese. "Empty hand" refers to the ability of karate students to defend themselves without the use of weapons. Karate consists of basic techniques that block or avoid an attack, and then a counterattack of the opponent by punching, kicking, striking, or any combination of these. O'Sensei[2] explains that karate teaches students to develop fast, powerful punches and kicks, as well as skills in joint manipulation and throwing. (The characters at the left, from top down, are *kara*, *te* and *do. Empty-hand way.*)

Karate may mean different things to different people. Young people often take up karate because they want to learn how to defend themselves. Elderly people, on the other hand, may only be looking  for an interesting and fun way to stay fit. Parents often enroll their children in karate lessons to teach them discipline and to develop their coordination. Karate is also a very good way to learn much about the culture of Japan as well as the culture of other countries.

Karate originated as a system of unarmed self-defense using only the hands, feet, and body of the practitioner. Karate as a means of self-defense training is based on scientific principles and knowledge of the working muscles and joints, and the relationship between movement and balance. This allows the student

2 Teruyuki Okazaki, member of the Japanese Karate Association and student of Gichin Funakoshi.

of karate to be prepared, both physically and mentally, to defend himself successfully against any attacker.

Karate as a physical art form is almost without equal. It provides fantastic all-around exercise and develops coordination and agility. In addition to its usefulness in self-defense, it is especially useful in keeping in good shape. It is widely practiced by both children and adults as a means of keeping in top physical condition. O'Sensei promotes traditional karate as a physical art among his students.

Karate's Storied Past

There are many legends concerning the origin of karate, and for the most part, historians still ponder the possibilities. It is clear, however, that modern karate as we presently know it is only a couple of hundred years old. The karate we practice today was developed in

Okinawa. For hundreds of years, it was influenced by the Chinese, who had been practicing various styles of *chuan fa* (a Chinese martial art often referred to as kung fu) for centuries. Through trade and exploration, these styles were introduced to Okinawa and ultimately intertwined with the Okinawan styles. In 1922, Gichin Funakoshi brought the fighting style of Okinawa to Japan, where it was christened *karate*.

Daruma Bodhidarma

A popular legend surrounding the spread of the martial arts centers on Daruma Bodhidharma, who traveled from India into China in the sixth century. Along with his spiritual message, he brought a physical set of exercises, which formed the basis of the famed fighting style of the Shaolin monks.

Bodhidharma was born a prince in the southern regions of India and raised as a warrior to succeed his father as king. He had been trained in the martial arts. Bored with his training, Bodhidharma began to study with a Buddhist teacher. On his deathbed, his teacher asked him to go to China to reawaken the followers of Buddha.

Legend has it that Bodhidharma traversed the Himalayan Mountains and arrived in China around AD 526. He set out in a northerly direction crossing the Tse River and reached the Sung Mountain range, where the Shaolin temple was located. It had been founded forty years earlier by Buddhist monks. Bodhidharma sought entrance into the Shaolin temple. He was accepted only after he was able to prove that he was committed to Buddhism by demonstrating his spiritual enlightenment through prolonged meditation.

Legend has it that Bodhidharma then went to a cave and stared at a wall for seven years. He is said to have cut off his eyelids to stay awake in meditation, and so is usually depicted with bulging eyes. Others say that he cut off his eyelashes and that they fell to the ground and became tea plants. Recognizing the ability of tea to help a person stay awake has made tea a part of the practice of zazen, a seated position of meditation used to develop spiritual enlightenment.

When he arrived, Bodhidharma was shocked to find the monks were fat and without the ability to stay awake during his lectures. The monks were unarmed and were easy victims for bandits when they attempted to go out and teach throughout the land. Some of them were so afraid; they decided to stay in the safety of the monastery. This was one reason Buddhism was no longer as well-known as it had been.

Bodhidharma created an exercise program for the monks that involved physical techniques imitating different animals. Eventually this type of training created the famous martial art of kung fu. After several years, the Shaolin monks became famous as great fighters and defenders of the people. These skills helped the monks to defend themselves against invading warlords and bandits. Bodhidharma taught that martial arts should be used for self-defense and never to hurt or injure needlessly. In fact, one of the oldest Shaolin sayings is "One who engages in combat has already lost the battle."

Bodhidharma also taught medicine to the monks and arranged for Chinese doctors to come to share their knowledge with the Shaolin. In three years, the monks became so skilled in both the martial arts and medicine that they came to be feared and respected by the bandits. This went a long way toward continuing the spread of Buddhism and Zen3 throughout China and the rest of Asia.

The death of Bodhidharma is shrouded in mystery. Legend has it that he was poisoned by one of his followers disappointed at not being selected as the successor. Regardless of the reason, Bodhidharma died in AD 539 at the Shaolin temple at age fifty-seven. He was laid to rest in a tomb there.

---

3 O'Sensei is a master teacher. Usually an "O" is used before the word *Sensei* to indicate respect.

The strangest legend regarding Bodhidharma is that three years later, he was met on the road by a government official, walking out of China toward the Himalayas with his staff in his hand and one of his sandals hanging from it. Having dined with Bodhidharma on many occasions, the official was certain it was him. When the official arrived at the monastery and recounted his experience, the monks opened the tomb only to find it contained just a single sandal.

The forms created and taught to these monks are generally believed to be the root of the martial arts in China. While there is evidence portions of these movements existed prior to the arrival of Bodhidharma, it was he who organized and recorded them. From there, they have gone on to spread throughout the world.

From China, it is believed the rudimentary components of martial arts were introduced to Okinawa. They were solidified into the basis of modern karate during the early Japanese occupation of the Ryukyu Islands as a means of self-defense. As the Okinawans were not allowed to perform their martial arts, its practice was done in secrecy. Following the dismantling of the Sho Monarchy of Okinawa in 1879, the practice of karate came out into the open. While the Bodhidarma is generally associated with the early origins of karate, its spread to Japan and the rest of the world is unanimously credited to Gichin Funakoshi, who was invited by the Royal Emperor of Japan to give demonstrations of the art form in the early twentieth century. It was the Japanese who applied the name *karate* to the style and later introduced it to the world.

Grandmaster Gichin Funakoshi,
father of modern karate

Gichin Funakoshi

The man most responsible for the systemization of traditional karate as we know it today was Gichin Funakoshi. He was born in Shuri, Okinawa, in 1869. When only a boy of eleven, he began to study karate under two top masters of the art at that time. In time, he became a karate master instructor and an expert in his own right. He is credited with being the first man to introduce karate to Japan proper, when he gave exhibitions in 1917 and again in 1922 at a physical fitness exposition sponsored by the Japanese Ministry of Education. The art soon caught on in Japan, and Funakoshi traveled throughout the country giving lectures and demonstrations. The main universities invited him to help them set up karate teams, and hundreds of people studied the art under his guidance.

In 1957, Master Funakoshi, the father of modern karate, passed away at the advanced age of eighty-eight. Tens of thousands of karate men who learned under him remain, ensuring that the art that he taught will not die with him. Today students all over the world are learning karate, which has become a world art.

Tora no Maki

Master Funakoshi's first book, *Ryukyu Kempo: Tode*, was edited by Bukyo-Sho in 1922. It included a series of prologues written by some of the most famous people in Japan and Okinawa at that time. On the cover of this book, a famous artist friend of Gichin

Funakoshi, Hoan Kosugi, placed the tiger symbol that later would come to symbolize Master Funakoshi's karate.

Hoan Kosugi was inspired by the Japanese saying *Tora no Maki*, which is a phrase that describes an official document established as a reference on a system. So *Ryukyu Kempo* would be the *Tora no Maki* of *Tode* (translated as "Chinese hand," a term for fist fighting used in early Okinawa). He also felt that Master Funakoshi gave the appearance of a feline due to his way of acting and his movements.

Chapter Two — The Masters

Hi! My name is Diana Linda Michele. I am fourteen years old; I will be fifteen years old on October 1, 2012.

I have a twin brother. His name is Roberto Marcus. I live in the San Joaquin Valley, near Madera, California.

I like all kinds of sports, but my favorite is traditional karate. My brother and I have been studying for six and a half years.

Master Vincent Cruz

My teacher is Master Vincent A. Cruz. He has practiced traditional karate for more than fifty years.

Master Hidetaka Nishiyama

Master Cruz's teacher was Grandmaster Hidetaka Nishiyama; and in turn, Master Nishiyama's teacher was Grandmaster Gichin Funakoshi.

The Rules of Behavior in Karate

Teachers in Japan are called sensei. So from now on, I will call my teacher O'Sensei in this book. The "O" before sensei means that my teacher is a senior master teacher; it is a badge of respect.

Karate is a martial art. You need to know that it requires a lot of discipline. You need to pay attention to what you are doing. You have to do things over and over until you get it right. O'Sensei tells me that practice makes perfect.

There are rules you must know before you start practicing karate. The first rule is that karate begins with respect and it ends with respect. Another important rule is that karate should only be used in self-defense and only when there are no other options. You must never use karate to intentionally injure or hurt someone else. If you have the opportunity to not fight, always choose to simply walk away from trouble. Remember, karate is a martial art and a fighting system. With it, we can cause serious damage to others (and ourselves if we are not careful). It is easy to break a finger when we punch if our fists are not clenched tightly. Once I lost my temper and hit a boy who was teasing me—right in the nose. O'Sensei was not amused, and I had to sit out of karate for the rest of class (not to mention that I had to apologize to the boy who teased me!).

It is the custom in karate for students to wear white uniforms. This is not to say it is wrong if you happen to see someone with a different color than white. O'Sensei tells me that our uniform is our outward appearance in karate. It should be kept clean; the uniform should always be folded and tied with your ranking belt. Since I am in traditional karate, our formal color belts are white, three degrees in brown, and five degrees in the black belt. There are other colors of belts between white and brown, and they signify advancement at different levels. They include yellow, orange, blue, purple, and green. The colors are used as levels of promotion as students get better. The levels of brown belt show how students are becoming strong martial artists and preparing to become black belts.

When you become a black belt, you are really just beginning your journey of mastery of karate. Each level of mastery is called a degree. As you get stronger and develop better technique, you move to a higher degree. In many systems, there are as many as ten degrees of black belts. Since you learn most of the technique during the first five degrees, the last five are given for complete mastery of the system and for years of continuous and careful examination of your karate.

Most karateka (someone who practices karate) keep their original black belt and if possible use it all of their lives. You can always tell someone who has trained a long time because the black belt is often faded and frayed.

Chapter Three — Basic Concepts

There are a few karate principles you need to know before we begin. They form the basis for all karate and all karate training. I will talk a little about each. The four most basic parts of training are:

- *Kihon* (basic techniques);
- *Kata* (form or pattern);
- *Bunkai* (study of techniques encoded in kata or "kata application"); and
- *Kumite* (sparring or paired form)

基本 — Kihon

Kihon means "basics" or "fundamentals"; it is by far the most important part of the art of karate. Without strong basic techniques, we cannot hope to perform effective karate. O'Sensei's teacher, Master Nishiyama, was regarded as one of the greatest karateka because his basic techniques were of a standard many of us can only dream of achieving.

Traditional karate is famous for giving its practitioners a strong kihon. In kihon, you learn the karate way of punching, blocking, kicking, and body movement. Often you will do drills for your sensei that may be monotonous and boring; however, you should always try your absolute best and snap out your blocks, punches, and kicks. I always work out this way because the way

A traditional karate training session will involve hundreds of repetitions of different punching action. It may take a class of beginners an hour to reach a point in the lesson where they actually punch using both arms at once. Kicking is also very important in traditional karate. The student is required to learn the different basic kicking techniques and spend many hours practicing. Kihon is not just a "beginners" exercise. It is practiced throughout your karate training, from white belts to the highest-ranking black belts.

型 — **Kata**

In *kata*, you learn to combine the basic techniques in a flowing movement. Each kata is built around a specific fighting strategy for you to understand. Always remember to look where you're going, and remember what you learned in kihon.

分解 — **Bunkai**

Bunkai literally means "analysis." In bunkai, you analyze every movement in a given kata and develop possible applications in real combat situations. Bunkai is a transition step to kumite. A single *kata* may be broken into anywhere from a few to a few dozen applications, and the same sequence of kata moves may sometimes be interpreted in different ways, resulting in several bunkai. This allows the student to understand what the movements in kata are meant to accomplish. For example, if an opponent threw a punch toward your face, you would need to defend with a block for a high punch. The same would be true for a kick or some other strike. By practicing kata, you learn to put combinations of blocks, punches, or kicks together that make sense in a real situation. Bunkai helps you to understand what your opponent is doing and how you are reacting. It may also illustrate how to improve techniques by adjusting distances, executing proper timing, and adjusting a technique depending on the size of an opponent. O'Sensei requires his students to perform bunkai for promotion.

組手 — **Kumite**

In *kumite*, you learn to apply kihon and bunkai in a controlled environment. When you train in kumite in a dojo, there are rules to follow so no one gets hurt. You train to control your strikes so contact with your opponent is not made. Punches and kicks are hard; however, with practice you learn to stop them short of hitting your partner. Both opponents are trying to score points, not hurt one another. While I like kumite very much, this is where I lost my cool and hit the boy who was making fun of me.

Kumite is one step toward real combat because two students will attempt to perform moves on each other and learn how the techniques really work. There are many forms of kumite. They include taking turns, or ippon juji kumite, which is another step toward free fighting. Remember to be calm, and don't worry about or pay any attention to how big and strong your opponent is. Sparring is a lot of fun; however, once in a while, you may be hit. So don't be afraid of getting hit. That will happen often, and it might hurt a bit. Most importantly, don't lose your cool! Your sensei will not like it if you do.

Training is a lot of fun, but it is also hard work. You must be dedicated and train every day if possible if you want to be good at karate. I have been lucky to have such a caring teacher and wonderful dojo to perform my karate in. Still, I train hard and do the basics every day.

空手着 — **Karate-Gi**

Karate-gi is the Japanese name for the karate training uniform. For beginners, the cut of the uniform is generally light and loose-fitting due to the nature of karate training. The karate-gi has evolved in a manner that maximizes mobility and speed. Most quality karate-gi are cut from a light canvas-style cloth, which will stand up to a considerable amount of abuse without restricting the mobility of the karateka. Typically, such a karate-gi is made of cotton canvas and can stand up to more rigorous applications.

The advanced student seems to favor the use of a heavier fabric. Despite the extra weight of the heavier fabrics, I prefer them due to their strength and the ability of the thicker fabric to wick away perspiration. It is not unusual for a martial artist to feel better cooled when using a heavier karate-gi.

The karate-gi is made of various colors depending on what school and style of karate you are studying. In my school, we prefer to wear the white gi.

気合 — Kiai, the Yell

Have you ever seen someone doing karate? Sometimes that person will yell or make a loud sound during practice or doing a form called a kata. O'Sensei explains that the yell is called *kiai*. He says that kiai is a short yell that comes from the stomach. He says that it is an inner burst of energy that helps us execute a strong karate technique. In karate, one must always remember we are using our "internal energy" as well as our physical strength to get the most out of our technique.

O'Sensei says that kiai helps me to project my own internal energy and strength. I do this by good breathing and timing. A relaxed and powerful lungful of air can add power to my movements. Kiai is used in all martial arts. The kiai can also be used to take physical advantage by scaring and discouraging your opponent. It should not be used on every technique, but instead, learn to build up your drive to execute the kiai at important moments, such as a finishing strike.

Chapter Four: Basic Principles

決め — Kime (Focus)

Kime is a Japanese martial arts term. In karate, it means "power" or "focus" of a technique so that everything occurs at the correct moment during the technique. The tension at this time is mostly focused in the tanden (strength center of the body located just below the navel and stretching to just above the pubic area). According to Japanese martial arts philosophy, energy called "ki" is stored in this area of the abdomen, also called the "hara."

The purpose of kime is an explosive focused attack to the target using the appropriate techniques and maximum power in the shortest time possible. Kime may be accomplished in striking, punching, and kicking, as well as in blocking. A technique lacking kime can never be regarded as true karate, no matter how great a resemblance it demonstrates to karate. A contest is no exception; however, it is against the rules to make contact because of the danger involved. So how do we spar? By training with control of our strikes and blocks and understanding distance. That's right! We learn to punch, kick, and block with full force—but just before we strike our target, we stop the strike. It takes a lot of practice to learn this, but it is necessary as we must always be mindful of hurting someone or getting hurt ourselves.

Power and Speed

O'Sensei emphasizes that karate would be useless without kime. Kime is the ability to concentrate the greatest amount of force at the point of attack. Students who do extremely well in karate do so by increasing their muscular power through kime. In addition, the student's power is directly related to the speed of his techniques. However, O'Sensei reminds us that speed is unsuccessful without proper body control, body concentration, and relaxation of power. The student cannot generate maximum power if his punches rely on the arm's muscles alone or his kicks on the leg's muscles alone. The maximum level of power comes from concentrating all of the student's strength from every part of the body, focused on the target. Maximum power is required only at the point of impact.

Speed comes with conditioning and repetition of properly performed techniques. It is a product of intense concentration and, at the same time, total relaxation of the body. Through dedicated practice and gradual understanding of how the body and mind work together, speed of properly executed technique is slowly developed.

To strengthen muscle power, the student must not only understand the principles of kihon; he or she must also give them effect with strong, elastic muscles. Strong muscles demand constant, serious training. O'Sensei also requires the student to know which muscles to use in his or her techniques; well-trained muscles will lead to strong and effective karate.

Rhythm and Timing

In karate, we call each punch, kick, strike, or block a technique. Techniques work in combinations. Sometimes they are in reaction to something someone else did, or on some occasions you have initiated the technique. Karate has its own rhythm, and the student should become aware of this and understand why. No technique takes place in isolation. In combining basic techniques, the student should pay attention to the timing of his or her techniques as well as the techniques themselves. For example, when an opponent moves toward you with a punch, there are many things you might do. Depending on the situation, you may just block and move away. You may block and return a punch, or if advanced enough in your training, you may move out of the way of the punch and have no contact at all.

O'Sensei tells us our movements not only contain a great deal of power but also rhythm and in their own way, beauty. O'Sensei reminds us that a sense of rhythm and timing will help us understand the techniques and the art of karate in general.

Hips

The hips are very important in karate. Many students often neglect this principle in executing karate techniques. Hip rotation adds power to the upper body, and it is important to strong blocks and punches. The hips' closeness to the body's center of gravity makes them the foundation of strong, stable movements, good balance, and proper form. The student cannot move as smoothly, quickly, or powerfully if the hips are inactive. For this reason, O'Sensei often reminds us to "block with your hips," "punch with your hips," and "kick from your hips."

Breathing

The student should coordinate his or her breathing with the techniques. Breathing enhances the karateka's ability to relax and concentrate maximum power in his or her techniques. Correct breathing—properly exhaling when finishing a strike, for example—is necessary to developing kime. Proper inhaling fills the lungs completely. Proper exhaling leaves the lungs about 20 percent full; while exhaling completely makes the body limp, leaving the student vulnerable to even a weak attack.

腹— Hara

Generally speaking, *hara* 4 means *belly*, but in the martial arts it means more specifically the lower part of the stomach, two inches below and under your belly button. This is your center of gravity. Without a stable center of gravity, you cannot maintain a good balance and techniques with weight behind them. In order to keep the center of gravity in the lower part of the abdomen, one has to learn abdominal breathing, which means up-and-down movement of the diaphragm.

Abdominal breathing has the added advantage of a soothing effect on your mind. When you are shocked or upset, the center of gravity tends to rise, causing shallow breathing, affecting the shoulders and

4 Zen, an art form of meditation.

chest. You can reverse this and become calm, forcing the center of gravity to the hara with stomach breathing. There are a few Japanese expressions showing the importance of this controlled breathing: "have a great will" means "broad-minded," and "to think will" means think rationally with the minimum participation of emotion.

引手 — Hikite, the Withdrawing Hand

O'Sensei teaches that the withdrawing hand leads the rotation of the hips. When executing a technique, the withdrawing hand must move strongly and quickly. If not, the technique will not reach its maximum effectiveness. Another important point is that both arms must move at exactly the same time. If you punch with the right hand, it is usual for the left elbow to be drawn straight back at the same time. This is called *hikite*.

気 — Ki, the Life Force

What is *ki*? *Ki*, pronounced like "key," translates as *life force* or *vital energy*. Ki is the energy of all living things, the living force of the universe. Nature is the ultimate source for health of mind, health of body, balance, and harmony. This key is the link between life and the living forces of nature and the universe, which are the foundations for balance. Balance and harmony are the essential elements of life.

O'Sensei says that the tanden is the container of the hara and the hara is the storage area of the ki. A good exercise of hara is breathing with your diaphragm. This type of breathing is practiced in karate. The inhaled air is pressed down to your lower center of gravity.

Life is energy. Every living thing has atoms and molecules in constant motion. O'Sensei told me that when the atoms spin clockwise, I am very healthy. When they spin counterclockwise, I could become tired and sick.

The "life force body" is the flow of the Creator in us. It gives life to the physical body. Without it, we would die. The life force body or heavenly body is an exact replica of the physical body. It flows along definite invisible "wires" or pathways called *meridians.*

Where there is pain or disease, there is a blockage of energy. Sometimes there is a surplus of energy that weakens the system. When the meridians are opened up, our bodies have an innate ability to heal themselves. We are always going toward homeostasis—back to balance.

Chapter Five — Philosophy

The Philosophical Mind

Before we continue, I need to explain certain philosophical principles that are very important in the art of traditional karate. O'Sensei explains that because of Master Funakoshi's teachings and karate philosophy, karate training became more meaningful for those who seriously practiced and made an effort to understand its deeper meaning.

As a result, karate today has become a highly scientific art. It makes the most effective use of all the parts of the body for defensive purposes and also includes the mind. We must learn to use our minds in our practice of karate. Here are a few basic principles to keep in mind.

Mizu no Kokoro

There is a term that the Japanese use to define calmness. It is called *mizu no kokoro*. *Mizu* means *water*, and *kokoro* is the *mind*. The first thing that *mizu no kokoro* implies is that when water is calm, there are no waves. There is no disturbance. The surface of an ocean appears perfectly still. O'Sensei explains that this is how we should aim to make our mind: perfectly still, calm, and relaxed.

In more practical terms, this particular state of *mizu no kokoro* is able to show calmness in the face of danger. It is the mind unperturbed by events and the stresses of life and is a great way to train yourself to remain calm.

Tsuki no Kokoro

Tsuki no kokoro (mind/spirit like the moon) is understood to mean a calm, clear mind not paying attention to any one thing—yet at the same time clearly aware of everything taking place in the surroundings.

正座 — **Seiza**

Seiza, literally *proper sitting*, is the Japanese term for the traditional formal way of sitting in the martial arts. To sit seiza-style, one first kneels on the floor, folding one's legs underneath one's thighs, while resting the buttocks on the heels. The ankles are turned outward as the tops of the feet are lowered so that, in a slight "V" shape, the tops of the feet are flat on the floor and big toes are overlapped, and the buttocks are finally lowered all the way down.

Depending on the circumstances, the hands are folded modestly in the lap or are placed palm down on the upper thighs with the fingers close together, or are placed on the floor next to the hips, with the knuckles rounded and touching the floor. The back is kept straight, though not unnaturally stiff. Traditionally, women sit with the knees together while men separate them slightly.

Some martial arts, notably kendo, iaido, and karate, may prescribe up to two fist widths of distance between the knees. Stepping into and out of seiza is mindfully performed. There are variations of the traditional method of entering and exiting the sitting position depending on occasion and type of clothing worn. It is also called the correct sitting form of meditation.

The Salutation-Seiza, Mokuso

At the beginning and end of each training class, we sit in the seiza posture. O'Sensei tells us that seiza is the correct formal sitting position in karate.

In the seiza position, O'Sensei asks us to assume the meditation position called Mokuso (pronounced "mohk-so"). Mokuso is performed before beginning a training session in order to clear one's mind.

This position also teaches us discipline. At first, it may be difficult to sit in this form. The position is awkward, and if done incorrectly, you can cut off the circulation to your feet. I have done this many times and believe me—it does not feel very good. But with practice, you will get used to it and sit very comfortably. O'Sensei tells us that mokuso does not mean "close your eyes." He says that it means to be still

23

or quiet and think and prepare oneself for an activity. So, it means to be quiet and contemplate.

Mokuso is something one does quickly to prepare oneself for an activity—for example, martial arts training or meditation. With practice, one can do mokuso instantly.

Rei, — Formal Bow

It is from seiza that the more formal bows of respect take place at the beginning and at the end of every class. This is called *rei*. It is

a formal bow used by all martial artists in Japan. This is the way to salute your sensei as well as the other students. This shows that you have respect for others as well as self-respect. More than just bowing at the be-ginning and the end of each class, rei also means saluting your classmates. Your sensei may ask you to pay respect as well to other guests visiting your school (called a *dojo*).

Master Gichin Funakoshi, the founder of traditional karate, left us Twenty Precepts to guide us in our training in karate. My personal favorite is number one, which to me says it all:

"Do not forget that karate begins and ends with rei."

Now you know why karate involves so much bowing. The reason is really quite simple. It is all about courtesy and respect.

渋み — **The Law of Shibumi**

Shibumi is a Japanese word that refers to a particular artistry of simple, subtle, and modest beauty. Like other Japanese artistic terms, shibumi can apply to a wide variety of subjects, not just art or fashion. O'Sensei says that shibumi can also apply to the martial arts. The principles of shibumi describe beauty and understanding the principle of living in perfect harmony with everything about us. O'Sensei's philosophy or teachings are entwined with righteous behavior as a karateka as well as a human being. O'Sensei applies the basic principles of shibumi into a basic law for his young students to follow. This law is repeated daily during the opening of a class session. He calls this:

Family

O'Sensei explains that family is the first and most important asset a student should consider. Nurturing the importance of the parents/student relation simply engrains and motivates the student's consciousness. The student respects this law by simply showing his deep love and respect for his parents. He begins to believe that family is nurturing his complete existence.

School

After the nurturing of family, the student's next duty is to consider the importance of school. She is required to recognize the importance of an education. She realizes her upcoming future when Mom and Dad are no more. Her only comfort is to depend on her profession through her years of school. She will also become a parent someday, and she will pass on these important precepts to her children.

Karate

The student learns that he must take care of his body through healthy conditioning. He may choose other physical conditioning practices. He may play football or tennis. He might take up golfing or fencing. However, since he is being taught the principles in a martial art environment, he may choose the latter.

How does the student achieve the Law of Shibumi? O'Sensei says that the student does not achieve it; she discovers it.

Does this mean that one must learn a great deal to arrive at shibumi?

Rather, it means that one must pass through knowledge and arrive at simplicity.

The Go-Jo

Bushido means "the way of the warrior." It grew out of the combination of Buddhism and Shintoism. In bushido, *bu* means

"martial," *shi* means "warrior," and *do* means "the way." The way of the samurai placed five rules of conduct to develop the spirit of the warrior. These were the essential studies of the bukyo and shido, as shown in the seven virtues of the warrior.

The Masters called five of these virtues the Go-Jo:

1. Chi	Wisdom and prudence
2. Gi	Justice, righteousness, honor, fidelity, duty, devotion, and attitude
3. Jin	Beatitude, dignity, and quality
4. Rei	Etiquette, ceremony, and just behavior
5. Shi-Yu	Heroic courage, superior consciousness

武道 — **Budo**

Budo is a Japanese term that characterizes the philosophy of the fighting spirit of those who practice it. It is used to denote the warrior culture (samurai) of Japan during their medieval history. In English, it is used almost exclusively in reference to Japanese martial arts.

The origin of Japanese martial arts can be found in the combatant customs of the samurai and the class system that controlled the use of weapons by members of the non-warrior classes.

Originally, samurai were expected to be expert in many weapons, as well as unarmed combat, and achieve the highest possible mastery of combat skills for the purpose of glorifying either themselves or their lord or sovereign. Over time, this purpose gave way to a way of life of achieving spiritual goals by trying to perfect their martial art skills. Thus, we have bushido, the way of the samurai.

Literally translated, *bushido* means "way of the warrior." More correctly, it was the moral code that the samurai of Japan were supposed to live their lives by.

Bushido was a tradition, a philosophy. As such, while the concept of bushido was fitting to all samurai, the details of the belief differed from clan to clan, and even from person to person. The precepts ranged from short (only three virtues are mentioned in Hagakure) to long (some had a hundred items). A standardized essay on bushido was never created.

Although there was no set list of the rules of bushido, there were seven characteristics (the seven virtues of the Gojo) that were common to most families. They are simple enough to remember, and yet provide some insight into the philosophies of the bushi (warriors).

Over time, two trends defined the arts: First, there was increasing specialization, and second, many of the arts evolved toward more peaceful practices and took on the teachings of budo, which implies a higher purpose than just the mastering of arms.

道場 — the Dojo

Dojo literally means "place of the Tao" in Japanese. O'Sensei explains that Tao means the "way" or the "path." He uses the word "principles" or "a form of doctrine." O'Sensei usually and simply teaches Tao by the yin/yang symbol, where every action creates an opposite action that is thought to be natural and a necessary movement. This is true in karate and physics. When we punch (tsuki), we withdraw the other hand (hikite) at an equal velocity to maintain power and balance. O'Sensei explains that at one time, martial arts dojos were attached to temples in Japan because of their importance in the Japanese culture.

A traditional *dojo*, or karate school, is held in reverence by its members. Such schools have many Okinawan and Japanese symbols and traditions. Members consider martial arts a way of life and show deep respect to their school, the teacher, and each other.

The yin/yang symbol

Always respect your sensei as well as your fellow students.
A little respect goes a long way.

Chapter Six — Getting Started

Karate training is rigorous and can be hard on your body. Just as in other activities, such as sports and dance, you must warm and loosen the body before going all-out. In karate, we use all parts of the body. We must, therefore, be mindful to stretch properly and follow a regimen of exercises designed to help us so we prevent injuries, such as muscle strains and sprains. At our dojo, we start by loosening up from head to toes. Standing in a natural position with legs spread apart (shoulder width) and hands on hips, we begin with circular movements of our head and gradually work our way from neck to shoulders, hips, knees, and ankles. The idea is to loosen all of our major joints before doing more physically demanding "strength exercises."

Calisthenics

O'Sensei says that calisthenics are an essential part of any athletic training and more so in karate. They are very useful in the development of all the mobile parts of the body. They are used for limbering up, muscle training, and improving your breathing. There are many different calisthenics exercises; however, for the sake of space in this book, I have selected my favorite exercises.

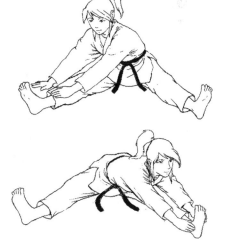

The Stretcher

The stretcher! This is a wonderful exercise for your back and legs. I do this exercise often, even when I am watching television at home. It helps to strengthen the muscles of your back, including your legs and arms. Your tummy also gets a workout. Sit on the floor with your legs spread apart as far as you can. Keep your back straight and reach toward one foot at a time and grab the foot pulling yourself forward. Maintain the described posture and feel the stretch. Slowly pull back, relax, and repeat the same procedure with the opposite leg.

The Famous Push-Ups

I like to warm up with push-ups. It is an excellent way to strengthen the upper body. Start with a few repetitions until you can do fifty repetitions and more. For best results, keep your back and knees straight and your weight balanced over your arms and shoulders.

Crunches

This exercise strengthens my back and super-strengthens my stomach muscles. It also exercises and builds the back of the legs and thighs. These exercises are difficult and require constant effort. It is common to feel the "burn" of the exercise, but with repetition, you will quickly get used to it and actually look forward to this element of your training.

Chapter Seven: Organizing the Karate Techniques

A "technique" in karate refers to a movement or positioning of the body in a way that allows you to take defensive maneuvers (whether being attacked or not) or initiate an offensive movement toward an opponent. Techniques include stances, body posturing, blocks, punches, strikes, kicks, and movements to "get out of the way." When done in clusters or more than one at a time, they are referred to as "combinations." We must learn the various techniques in an orderly and organized way. Each technique builds on another. They are connected in a way that, through careful and continuous practice, you can apply them without much conscious thought. By grouping the techniques in an organized fashion, the proper transition from one to another is made much easier and, therefore, more effective.

Here is a list of techniques we will be studying in this book. Both the English explanations and Japanese terms used in traditional karate are provided. These are always useful when attending other schools or competitions. Some schools teach entirely in English, while others use the Japanese terms only.

Stance Techniques

Stance is an important element in karate. A strong and well-executed technique of both defense and attack depends to a large extent on a balanced and stable stance. The various stances are based on the two factors of strength and agility. They are:

Informal attention stance (Heisoku-dachi)

Open leg stance (Hachiji-dachi)

Straddle leg stance (Kiba-dachi)

Straddle leg stance (Shiko-dachi)

Forward stance (Zenkutsu-dachi)

Back stance (Kokutsu-dachi)

Cat-foot stance (Neko ashi dachi)

Diagonal straddle stance (Sochin-dachi)

Wide hourglass stance(Hangetsu-dachi)

T-Stance (Renoji-dachi)

Rooting stance (Fudo-dachi)

Posture Techniques

Posture techniques have to do with the positioning of the body in relation to an intended target. These techniques can be performed from any of the above-listed stances and are intended to make the application of a technique more efficient. Posture techniques can be used for defense as well as for attacking or counterattacking.

Front facing (used mainly in attacking; shoulders are parallel to the target)

Half front facing (used mainly in defense; shoulders face target at forty-five-degree angle)

Side facing (used in both defense and attack; shoulders are perpendicular to the target)

Shifting Techniques

Shifting techniques refer to "tai sabaki" or body shifting. By using these techniques you are essentially doing one of two things: (1) you are shifting your body position to more effectively deliver a strike, or (2) you are using the technique as a defense to "sidestep" an opponent's movement, thereby moving out of the line of attack.

Stepping (used with the forward stance, diagonal straddle stance, or back stance) is shifting where a relatively large change of position is desired. This strategy may be used to change the distance between yourself and your opponent and is used for both offensive and defensive purposes.

Sliding is another shifting technique. By using the ground as a platform of initiation, you transfer your weight in the desired direction of movement without lifting the feet significantly. Although requiring considerable practice to master, this technique is invaluable in avoiding an attack and repositioning yourself for a counterstrike.

Basic Punching Techniques

Punching techniques involve the closed fist and are the most fundamental attacking technique used in karate. Karate punches use a straight punch technique with a twist of the wrist near the point of impact. This is called "furi." Always hit with your first two knuckles, and make sure that you focus, with powerful extension. Pull the fist that isn't punching back to your waist very quickly as you punch. This is called "hikite," and if timed correctly, will help your punch be stronger and sharper. A list of the most common punching techniques appears below.

Fore-fist straight punch (Seiken-choku zuki)

Lunge punch (Oui zuki)

Reverse punch (Gyaku zuki)

Spear-hand straight thrust (Nukite)

Vertical fist punch (Tate zuki)

Rising punch (Age zuki)

Roundhouse punch (Mawashi zuki)

Close punch (Ura zuki)

Double-fist punch (Morote zuki)

U-Punch (Yama zuki)

Hook punch (Kagi zuki)

Double punch (Morote tsuki)

Striking Techniques

Striking techniques differ from punching techniques in that they use other parts of the body besides the closed fist. With the open hand, the backhand, palm, fingers, both edges of the hand, as well as the elbows may be used to strike. Below is a list of the most common striking techniques.

Back fist strike (Riken-Uchi)

Bottom fist strike (tettsui-Uchi)

Backhand strike (Haishu-Uchi)

Knife-hand strike (Shuto-Uchi)

Ridge hand strike (Haito-Uchi)

Palm heel strike (Teisho-Uchi)

Elbow strike (Empi-Uchi)

Blocking Techniques

Blocking techniques are used primarily for defense and employ nearly every part of the body, including the legs and feet. They are used for protection and to establish a means for setting up counterattacks. Below are a list of the most common blocking techniques used.

Rising block (Age-uke)

Forearm block (Ude-uke)

Knife-hand block (Shuto-uke)

Downward block (Gedan barai)

X-Block (Juji-uke)

Wedge block (Kakiwake-uke)

Punching block (Tsuki-uke)

Palm heel block (Teisho-uke)

Chicken head wrist block (Keito-uke)

Bent wrist block (Kakuto-uke)

Backhand block (Haishu-uke)

Bottom fist block (Tetsui-uke)

Hooking block (Kake-uke)

Grasping block (Tsukami-uke)

Sweeping block (Nagashi-uke)

Pressing block (Osae-uke)

Scooping block (Sukui-uke)

Kicking Techniques

Kicking techniques involve the feet and legs. While they usually take longer to deliver, they are generally more powerful than other striking techniques. There are many different kicks in karate, but the most commonly used are:

Front kick (Mae geri) –hit with the ball of the foot

Side kick (Yoko geri) –hit with the blade of your foot, toes pointing down

Roundhouse kick (Mawashi geri) –hit with the ball of the foot; curl your toes up and try to turn your foot sideways

Stomping kick (Fumikomi geri)

Back kick (Ushiro geri) – this is a kick behind you; make sure you look where you're kicking and hit with the heel

Jumping front kick (Mae tobi geri)

Jumping side kick (Yoko tobi geri)

Crescent kick (Mikazuki geri)

Inside snapping kick (Nami ashi) – mostly used as a block

Chapter Eight: Stances

We will begin by getting familiar with some basic fundamentals. There are many stances in karate; however, in this book, we are going to learn the most basic stances required in learning karate. No one stance is more important than another. They each serve a specific purpose. Just as a foundation is necessary for a house to be strong,  so it is with karate. The stance creates a foundation for the execution of all techniques in karate. A strong stance is essential in the development of traditional karate. Stances provide stability during the execution of the basic techniques, as well as a means to transition from one technique to another. Without a strong and well-balanced stance, offensive and defensive techniques will not be as effective as they might possibly be. Insert K55.jpg to right.

O'Sensei makes me practice in place, moving forward and backward, up and down on the floor. As I got better, he had me move in different directions, combining different stances in different situations. Traditional karate postures are practiced very low in order to strengthen and make flexible the legs and hips. Low positions really hurt and seemed awkward at first, but soon enough, I was able to produce stability and began to develop strong legs and hips.

O'Sensei teaches that there are two categories of positions, inside tension and outside tension. In inside tension stances, the knees are brought in one to the other; outside tension positions have the knees push away from each other. The stance and the tension in the muscles must provide stability to withstand the impact when executing a strike or receiving a blow. Stances also provide the support for balanced footwork.

The most commonly used stances in traditional karate are zenkutsu-dachi (front stance), kiba-dachi (horse or side stance), and kokutsu-dachi (back stance). Zenkutsu-dachi is the most commonly used, mainly because it is a position that is more natural to the human body, whose legs prefer to go forward and backward rather than sideways.

As you progress through the rankings toward shodan (first Dan black belt), progressively more emphasis is placed on getting stances perfected. There are many different stances and even more variations of individual stances than I will have time to talk about. Some are used in very specific and highly advanced techniques that are not often used, so I will save discussion of those for another time. Many stances, however, are used in our everyday training. We generally refer to these as "formal stances." They are the most important to learn and the ones O'Sensei wants me to talk about.

Here is a list of the twelve most basic and common stances with the formal Japanese name and the English translation:

1. Heisoku-dachi (Closed-foot stance): feet together, parallel, with toes pointing forward
2. Masubi-dachi (Stance of attention)
3. Heiko-dachi (Parallel stance)
4. Hachiji-dachi (Open leg stance): feet shoulder width apart, with toes pointed out at a forty-five-degree angle; also called *yoi* (ready) position
5. Kiba-dachi (Horse stance)
6. Shiko-dachi (Straddle leg stance)
7. Zenkutsu-dachi (Front stance)
8. Kokutsu-dachi (Back stance)
9. Sochin-dachi or Fudo-dachi (Diagonal straddle stance)
10. Neko ashi dachi (Cat-foot stance)
11. Renoji-dachi (T-Stance)
12. Sanchin-dachi (Rooting stance)

閉足立 — **Heisoku-Dachi (Closed-Foot Stance)**

Place your feet together. This is usually a transitional stance, although it is used as the ready stance in some kata.

O'Sensei says this stance is the "stance of peace." This stance lets the sensei know that you are ready to receive his instructions. You must be prepared in your mind and in your heart that you really want to learn karate.

Heisoku-dachi is formed by placing your feet together parallel with no distance between them (heels and toes and knees close together).

You must be very quiet and ready for your lesson.

結び立 — **Masubi-Dachi (Stance of Attention)**

Masubi-dachi is one of the most important stances in Shotokan. This is the position from which we bow, although many make the mistake of bowing from heisoku-dachi.

This is the position from which we first bow to a partner in kumite, showing him or her the utmost respect. This is the position you bow in when you enter the dojo, showing complete respect to the dojo and the sensei. And this is also the position from which you bow when you perform kata, paying absolute respect to the art itself. Notice in the illustration that while the heels are touching, the feet are angled or spread apart. This is an important distinction from heisoku-dachi.

This stance is imperative, and although very simple, it is fundamentally one of the most important stances in karate. The Twenty Principles teach, "In karate start with a bow and finish with a bow," and it is from this stance that we do this, highlighting its significance.

平行立 — Heiko-Dachi (Parallel Stance)

In heiko-dachi, the feet are at shoulder width, and their outer edges are parallel. The heels are also separated and not touching.

Also called musubi-dachi, it is done with open heels until both outer edges of the feet are parallel. This is a common transitional stance in many kata and self-defense stances.

This stance is not part of the karate techniques. Rather, it is a natural posture in everyday use. One of the aims of karate training is to enable the students to move into offensive or defensive maneuvers from these natural positions.

八字立 — **Hachiji-Dachi (Open-Leg Stance)**

This is a natural stance, literally "stand like the character 八." The feet are at shoulder width, toes open at about forty-five degrees. Sometimes this stance is called soto-hachiji-dachi (外八字立). This is the basic ready stance in karate.

After you have bowed to your sensei and to your classmates, your sensei will ask you to stand in the ready position. You will use this stance over and over in all your practices.

In hachiji-dachi, the feet are shoulder width apart, toes pointing forward. The karateka stands upright, facing straight forward. While in hachiji-dachi, the karateka is usually in a yoi (ready) position.

The yoi position is a preparatory position that gives a clear starting point for execution of other techniques. The main version of yoi means the arms are slightly moved forward, with fists closed. The fists point slightly to the center line and are roughly half a shoulder width apart. The elbows should be bent very slightly.

騎馬立 — **Kiba-Dachi (Horse Stance)**

In this stance, the heels are firmly planted on the ground, and toes are pointing straight ahead. Feet are parallel and wide; weight is central and low, with the back straight and the knees and feet pointing slightly inward. Spread your legs a distance of approximately two shoulder widths. Knees should be over the big toes. This stance is not used in all styles of karate because of the strong tension that it requires; instead, it is often replaced by shiko-dachi.

四股立 — **Shiko-Dachi**

This is known as the straddle leg stance. It is often called the horse stance where kiba-dachi is not used.

This stance is the same as kiba-dachi, except the toes face out at about forty-five degrees. It is a very comfortable stance. The difference between shiko and kiba dachi is the tension of the legs. In shiko the tension is outward, whereas in kiba-dachi, the tension tends to be inward. Both are basically very strong.

前屈立 — **Zenkutsu-Dachi (Front Stance)**

This is a long frontal stance where the weight is mostly on the front leg. It has the exact same height as shiko-dachi, but the rear leg is completely straight at the knee and extended back. The front foot is placed frontal (toes facing forward). The rear foot is turned out thirty degrees, but never ninety degrees as seems natural to new practitioners because this precludes any forward motion. The heel of the rear foot rests on the ground. Zenkutsu-dachi is one of the most common stances in kata.

45

後屈立 — **Kōkutsu-dachi (Back Stance)**

This is a mirror image of zenkutsu-dachi, where the rear leg is bent strongly at the knee and the front leg is completely straight. It should be noted that most shotokan practitioners practice a slightly bent front knee which results in a much more balanced and functional stance. The front foot is turned ninety degrees to the side. The body is turned ninety degrees or more away, except for the head. Kokutsu-dachi is a great defensive stance because of the amount of energy stored in the rear leg, ready for a counterattack.

不動立 — **Fudō-dachi is also called Sochin-dachi (Diagonal Straddle Stance)**

The body is positioned similar to shiko-dachi but turned either forty-five or ninety degrees to the side, except for the head, which still looks forward. The front foot moves forward approximately one foot-length, and by doing so, this increases body stability, thereby making it possible to perform a strong yoko-geri (roundhouse kick) with the rear foot. Again, it should be noted that many shotokan practitioners practice a slightly bent front knee. The front foot is turned ninety degrees to the side. Sochin-dachi is a great defensive stance because of the amount of energy stored in the rear leg, ready for a counterattack.

猫足立 — **Neko Ashi Dashi (Cat-foot Stance)**

This technique is very beautiful if it is executed correctly. The secret is keeping your body straight. Tense the rear leg so that it points diagonally. Keep your back foot flat on the floor to support your upper body. Bring your front leg close to the rear leg. Since the front leg barely supports the body weight, the leg is free to kick your opponent. It is a fast technique moving from a front stance to the cat stance.

This is a versatile stance. The front foot can be held in preparation for a front leg front kick; the stance can be used when someone attempts to sweep your front leg; and it can be used as a "transition stance" between other stances or when changing direction to face another opponent.

レの字立レ — **Renoji-Dachi (T-Stance)**

The renoji-dachi is a very high stance, well suited to transitory movements or in movements that are preparatory for other techniques.

O'Sensei explains that renoji-dachi is a kamae (fighting) stance. He says that the stance is similar to the Japanese fencing kendo and iaido ready stance.

In renoji-dachi, stand like the character to the left.

Feet are at shoulder width. The foot in front is fully frontal (toes facing forward); the rear foot is turned ninety degrees out and is positioned in such a way that if the front foot is brought back, its heel will touch the heel of the rear foot. Thus, the footprint is shaped like the character レ (or letter L). The weight is kept 70 percent on the rear foot.

The heels are aligned in this stance with the rear foot being turned outward to an angle of approximately ninety degrees, and the front foot pointing straight forward. Both the front and rear legs have only a slight bend, while approximately 60 to 70 percent of the weight is on the rear leg, which means that the hips must tilt slightly upward in the rear. When viewed from above, the hips are at a forty-five-degree angle. The hips are pressed forward and slightly rotated upward.

The back and head are held straight, with the abs tensed slightly. The head is held vertical and level, focused in the direction of travel. The shoulders are aligned with the hips in a forty-five-degree angle.

サンチン — **Sanchin-Dachi (Rooting Stance)**

This is a stance of inside tension, meaning that the knees are pushed inward. Begin by standing in heiko-dachi, with the feet one hip-width apart, turning the feet slightly inward. Move the left foot forward, so that the heel is in line with the toe of your right foot. Keep knees slightly bent. Tense the inner thighs and pull up through the hips. This stance is found in advanced katas.

Chapter Nine: Body Posturing and Shifting

Body posturing and *body shifting* are terms used to describe the positioning of the body while in a stance and preparing to execute a technique, as well as how you move from one position to another. Once again, there are many different positions and ways to do this, so I want to focus on some of the most important concepts. These are the ones we learn first and use every day.

Hamni — Half Facing Posture

I need to explain this very important principle. The half-facing position is meant to be relaxed, comfortable, and natural, and should in no way look or feel artificial or stiff. The body rotation should be smooth in the horizontal plane. From the correct hamni position, one can move readily in any direction. This body mechanic prepares the body for hip rotation. Your hip is coiled back and ready to exert generated, forceful hip power to the front. Usually this body mechanic is used to deliver a strike. It is also used in body defense by allowing fewer targets to your opponent.

Body Shifting

O'Sensei explains that shifting consists of stepping, sliding, turning, or a combination of these. He says that one should try to maintain balance at all times. Shifting the weight of the body should be done smoothly. Try to keep your hips in a straight line. Don't raise or lower your hip when executing a shifting technique. And most of all don't raise your feet high off the ground. On the other hand, do not drag your feet.

Stepping

With stepping, one foot moves to make up distance. The other foot remains stationary until the stepping foot completes its movement. The stationary foot then "slides" forward into position. This principle is true whether moving forward or away from an opponent. Always maintain strong balance. Be smooth as you step from one position to the other. Do not raise and lower your hips. They should move in a straight line. Don't raise your feet high off the ground. Your feet should move about one inch off the floor. It is tough, but I know you can do it with practice. Remember, practice makes perfect. This technique is used when performing the forward stance, straddle stance, or back stance.

Stepping forward in front stance

Stepping back from a back stance

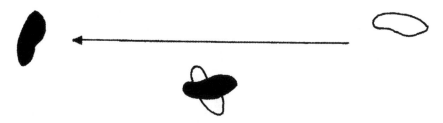

As above, keep your stationary foot solidly on the floor. Try to do this technique as smoothly as possible.

Yori Ashe –Shifting

This kind of "shifting" occurs when the feet slide across the floor to a new position, but the stance doesn't change. Generally the front foot moves first, and then the rear foot catches up. Shifting lets us move around the floor without giving up a strong fighting stance in order to take a step.

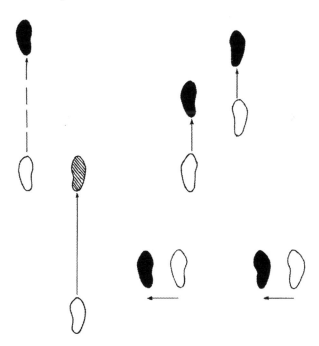

Amawate - Turning

These two turns are the most important 180-degree turns. They are done with the forward stance. However, they can be used with almost all fighting stances.

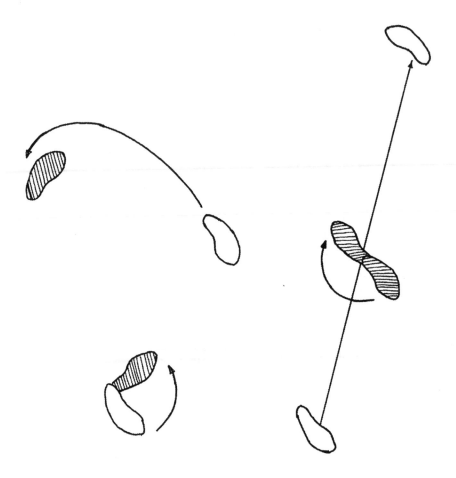

Kime - Focus

You might remember we spoke about kime in chapter four. It is  so important that I think it needs mention again. The essence of a karate technique is *kime*. Kime may be accomplished by striking, punching, or kicking, but also in blocking. The purpose of kime is to create an explosive focused attack to the target using the appropriate techniques and maximum power in the shortest time possible. To simply state it, kime means to time all of the components of a movement so that they occur together or at the most focused moment. A technique lacking kime can never be regarded as true karate, no matter how great a resemblance it demonstrates to karate.

A contest is no exception; however, it is against the rules to make contact because of the danger involved. So how do we spar? A concept called *sun-dome* means to arrest a technique just before contact to the target (one sun, meaning about three centimeters). But not carrying a technique through to kime is not true karate, so the question is how to reconcile the contradiction between kime and sun-dome. The answer lies in establishing the target slightly in front of the opponent's vital point. It can be hit in a controlled way with maximum power without making contact.

Chapter Ten: Punching Techniques

Punching techniques are often referred to as offensive techniques. The purpose of offensive techniques in karate is to render the attack of the opponent useless; therefore, they are not used against an opponent whose attack poses no threat. One of the unique features of karate is that attacking techniques can be used directly for blocking as well. This should be kept in mind in studying the following pages. The various forms of attacking by hand are broadly differentiated into punching and striking. The distinction between these will become clear from the examples shown.

Tsuki (zuki)

Punching techniques make use of the fore-fist, one-knuckle fist, fore-knuckle fist, palm heel, spear hand, and so forth. All the representative hand techniques based on the use of these striking points are both fast and effective. O'Sensei says that in basic practice, the punching hand should start from the ready position just above the hip bone; but for actual use, it must be trained to punch smoothly and effectively from any position.

(突き) *Tsuki* is the Japanese word for "thrust." In karate and its options, choku-zuki is the term used for "straight punch." The chamber, or preliminary position, of choku-zuki is with the striking hand retracted to the hip or ribs, in a fist, with the palm facing up. The punch travels in a linear path directly toward the target, with the elbow behind the fist, tracing the fist's path. The hand remains palm up until the last two inches of the punch, when it rotates to face down. This action is called "furi." Ideally, the beginning of the fist's rotation coincides with the initial contact with the target. Contact is made with the knuckles of the fore-fist. A straight punch executed from a front stance (zenkutsu-dachi) is called gyaku-zuki (reverse punch) if the advanced leg and fist are on opposite sides, or oi-zuki (lunge punch) if the leg and fist are on the same side. Gyaku-zuki, Shotokan karate's strongest punch, develops power through movement of the *hips*. The hips twist as the returning (nonpunching) hikite arm is pulled back and the punching arm is pushed forward, the fist twisting at point of impact. Tensing of the whole body is synchronized as the punch makes contact, and at this time, the rear foot is pushed down.

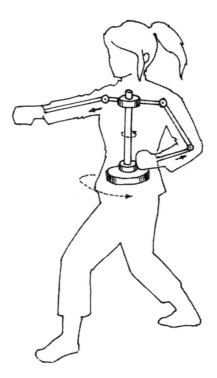

How to Make a Fist

Tightly clench the fingers in succession; finally, press the forefinger and middle finger down firmly with the thumb.

To begin, first open your hand.

Starting with the little finger, begin coiling your fingers.

Make sure your four fingers are tightly curled in the ball of your hand.

Tuck your thumb across the first two fingers to lock the fist..

In the beginning, the fist rests near the hip, with the palm facing upward. During the strike, the arm is extended forward in a straight line, and as the elbow passes the body and the wrist begins to twist, complete the punch so that the palm faces to the ground. The target is hit with the knuckles of the first two fingers (index finger and middle finger). This is seiken.

Only the knuckles of the index and middle fingers strike the target. The fist must extend straight from the wrist so that it does not bend over when it strikes. The wrist must be kept tense and unbent. The back of the hand and the wrist should form a straight line. The primary use is in the thrust punch (tsuki). The power of the arm must be concentrated and flow in a straight line to the knuckles

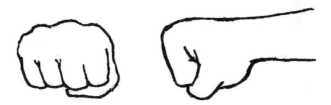

Elbow and Foot Techniques

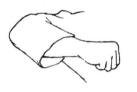

Empi (Elbow): Used mainly in attacking the chin, chest, solar plexus, and ribs. It is also used in closed-in blocking.

Koshi (Ball of Foot): Be sure to curl your toes upward as far as possible. Used in front and roundhouse kicking to attack the face, jaws, solar plexus, groin, ribs, and such.

Sokuto (Foot Edge): Used in side kicking and stomping to attack the face, armpits, solar plexus, and knees.

Kakato (Heel): Used in back kicking and stomping to the instep or shin and when attacking a fallen opponent to all the frontal body areas.

Haisoku (Instep): Used in front and roundhouse kicks. It is a very effective attack to the groin area.

Tsumasaki (Tips of Toes): Used for a front kick as a penetrating technique. Toes must be tucked and tighten for this execution.

Other Striking Techniques

Uraken-Uchi (back fist): Used is close-up fighting and effective to head or ribs.

Tettsui (Hammer fist): Fist is used as a hammer to attack the ridge of the nose, collarbone, back of the head, elbow joints, ribs, side of the face, and stomach area. It is also used in blocking

Seiryuto (Ox Jaw hand): Used mainly in blocking and in attacking the collarbone.

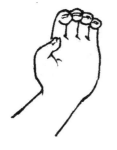

Teisho-(palm heel): Bend the wrist upward to form nearly a ninety degree angle. Used in attacking the face, chin, nose, jaw, solar plexus and in blocking.

Ippon ken (One-knuckle punch): Extend the knuckles of the forefinger out from a regular fist and hold down the thumb. Used in attacking the temple and the eyes.

Yonhon-Nukite (Spear hand): Make sure to make the ends of the three striking fingers flush. This technique is used in attacking the solar plexus, ribs, and chest.

Hiraken (Fore knuckle fist): Press the fingers together with the thumb. It is used in attacking the point between the nose and the upper lip, the temple, and the solar plexus.

Haishu (Back hand): This technique allows you to block as well as strike areas of the body.

Haishu Uke

Haishu Uke lets us knock an attack away using the back of our hand.

Chapter Eleven: Basic Punching Techniques

Now that we have a better idea of what a punching technique is and how we make an effective fist, here are some of the principal types of punching used in traditional karate:

- Age-zuki (上げ突き), rising punch
- Choku-zuki (直突き), straight punch
- Gyaku-zuki (逆突き), punch with the rear arm
- Kagi-zuki (鉤突き), hook punch
- Mawashi-zuki (回し突き), roundhouse punch
- Morote-zuki (双手突き), augmented punch using both hands
- Oi-zuki (追い突き), punch with the lead arm
- Tate-zuki (立て突き), vertical fist punch into the middle of the chest (short-range)
- Ura-zuki (裏突き), upside-down fist punch into solar plexus area (short-range)
- Yama-zuki (山突き) or Rete-zuki, two-level double punch (combination of ura-zuki and jodan oi zuki)
- Teisho uke palm heel block

Choku-zuki (直突き), Straight Punch

The first technique I learned in karate was how to punch the choku-zuki. *Choku-zuki* is the term used for "straight punch." I normally practiced this punch from heiko-dachi (natural stance), feet approximately shoulder width apart, toes pointing to the front, and

shoulders relaxed, head looking straight ahead. Remember to use the muscles of your stomach pushing down to activate the tanden. Your body weight should be evenly distributed over both left and right legs. One arm is placed straight out in front, with a fist formed. Remember to keep the shoulder of the punching arm relaxed and down and the back of the punching hand facing up.

When you start the punch, your right fist will start in the hikite position at the right of your body. The right punching arm starts to move straight forward, but nothing else moves. Keep the palm facing upward, and do not let the elbow wander away from the body; make sure you keep the elbow directly behind the fist throughout this karate move. When your elbow comes level with the front of your stomach, begin to rotate the right forearm counterclockwise; your forearm and fist should travel through 180 degrees and complete the twisting movement at the end of the punch. Be sure to keep the wrist straight and the two large knuckles facing forward.

At exactly the same time you are punching with the right hand, the left hikite arm, or pulling arm, which is out in front, begins to pull back to the hikite position at the side of your body. As soon as the pullback starts, twist the left arm ninety degrees counterclockwise, so that the bottom of the hikite fist is facing down, and then start to pull the arm back in a straight line. Once again, keep the elbow in a straight line. As soon as the elbow reaches the side of the body, the last ninety-degree rotation can be completed, and the left hikite arm will be palm up.

Remember that both arms should be moving at exactly the same time, and both left and right arms should stop at the same time (kime). Breathing should be silent, breathing out on the execution of this basic karate move.

When punching, the power is generated not only from the upper body and arms, but from the legs and with the hips, which initially rotate back to pull back the left reaction hand (hikite) and then immediately thrust forward at the completion of the punch, so the hips once again return to their starting position. This particular movement generates tremendous power in the punch. The muscles behind the thigh play a major part in the punch, and these muscles tense at the end of the move, along with the stomach muscles and the muscles beneath the right punching arm.

Oi-zuki (追い突き), Forward Punch

This is a very strong punch. O'Sensei says that this punch is the most used in karate. You notice that the punching hand is on the same side as the leg that moves forward. The force of the body moving forward is used to give strength to the punch. It is ordinarily used with the front stance (zenkutsu-dachi) and diagonal straddle stance (fudo-dachi). It is very effective in closing in on the opponent and delivers a strong attack.

A lunge punch quickly closes the distance between you and an attacker. If the attacker is taller and has a longer reach, the lunge punch will enable you to use in-close fighting techniques and eliminate your attacker's advantage.

Face forward with your feet about shoulders' width apart. Step forward on one leg with your knee bent. Your back leg will be straight (front stance). Drive your rear foot forward strongly. The same-side hand is held as an upturned fist at the side. Punch forward with the same-side hand as your rear foot lands forward. Pull your other hand back into an upturned fist at the side at the same time. This will add power to the punch. Retract your punch immediately to strike or defend in a guarded fighting position.

Gyaku-zuki (逆突き), Reverse Punch

A gyaku-zuki is a karate technique. It involves a punch executed by the back arm. A gyaku-zuki is sometimes called a "reverse punch." It is executed better if you use the hips to push it forward. It is one of the most used and effective punches used in a karate fight. The punch is generally to strike the solar plexus. The movement of a gyaku-zuki consists of muscles, such as the gluteus maximus, calf muscles, and thigh muscles. For long-range punches, twisting is important.

As stated by the Academy of Traditional Karate, Inc.: This is similar to the oi-zuki except that the opposite fist is used. Start in a zenkutsu-dachi (front-leg-bent stance) with the seiken (proper fist) of

the back leg chambered palm up, covering the ribs on that side of the body. The other arm is extended forward in a ready position with the elbow bent at a ninety-degree angle. The shoulders and hips are twisted slightly with the chambered side back, like a loaded spring. The punch starts by rotating and unwinding the hips to a full forward position, which unwinds the shoulders and launches the fist straight forward. The arm should slide straight forward along the ribs, like a piston, keeping the elbow against the body. The fist remains palm up until the elbow clears the body. Just before impact, the fist is snapped over, palm down."

Age-zuki (上げ突き), Rising Punch

O'Sensei teaches this punch with a little twist at the end. It is a combination between a small roundhouse punch and a rising punch. However, we cannot forget that it is a rising punch and that it must follow the rule of choku-zuki.

It is an excellent punch. The target is the head, nose, or chin. It can also be used to attack the side of the head using that little twist I told you about at the beginning. In order to gain power, use the hips, breathing with the deep diaphragm technique and kiai.

Remember, it is all in the breathing and focusing your technique.

Ura-zuki (裏突き), Close Punch

This is an effective form of attack in close-in fighting. It is important that you keep the elbows tucked close to your body. By doing this, you stay connected to your body. When you lose connection, you lose power. Also, using your hip, strong stomach (hara), and the muscles of the legs and buttocks will increase the power of this technique. This technique is executed in any stand. It is almost a hook punch, but the fist is in a perpendicular position. As I stated before, the power of this technique is in the hip and concentrated stance from the floor.

Mawashi-zuki (回し突き), Roundhouse Punch

This is a circular punch aimed at the opponent's temple and side of the face. It can also be used as a roundhouse punch to the side of the ribs. The fore-fist, fore-knuckles fist, or a one-knuckle fist may all be used as a striking point. As soon as the elbow leaves the body, the arm hooks in a semicircular movement toward the target.

This technique is usually performed as a reverse punch to take advantage of the twisting movement of the hips, but it may also be executed from the lunge punch.

Kagi-zuki (鉤突き), Hook Punch

Kagi-zuki is a very traditional technique, which received greater emphasis when karate was practiced as primarily an art of self-defense. Since the elbow is bent, the power is less, but it can be used effectively in close-range confrontation.

Like the roundhouse punch, the hook punch uses the index and middle knuckles of the fore-fist and takes a curving path to the target.

It is very important that you use the abdominal muscles. When the shoulder muscles contract, the punching hand leaves the ready position. The fist moves in a semicircle, and then changes to a straight path. Fist rotation takes place during the latter part of the movement. Try to use as many muscles as possible when executing this great technique.

71

Kisami-zuki, Jab Punch

This is a very popular attacking technique. Usually it is used with a follow-up technique like a reverse punch. It may be used with the front stance or back stance .In competition (kumite), it is usually executed with fudo-dachi (diagonal straddle stance).

The body is positioned similar to shiko-dachi, turned either forty-five or ninety degrees to the side, except for the head, which still looks forward. The front foot moves one foot-length forward, increasing stability and making it possible to perform the kisami-zuki. It is performed with a strong front kick with the rear foot.

Yama-zuki (山突き) or Rete-zuki

This two-level double punch is a combination of ura-zuki and oi-zuki)

Yama-zuki (the "mountain punch") is an excellent technique. It takes the name from its appearance. With one hand above and one below the head, arms and shoulders have a shape very much like the Japanese character *yama* (山, mountain).

This technique may be performed from any stance. The basic execution begins with both hands chambered or stacked up to the side of your body. With a striking force, your left hand executes a hook punch to the stomach; at the same time, a right hook punches the face.

Both punches must be delivered and land on the target at the same time, as you exhale through your mouth forcefully.

Morote-zuki (双手突き), Double-Fist Punch

This is a forward straight punch in which both hands strike at the same target at the same time. It is a very powerful technique that is difficult to block. Both fists begin from the hips and end to the front attacking the chest area. This technique may be executed in the front stance; however, it can be used from a standing stance and stepping forward attack using the principle of furi when executed.

Chapter Twelve: Striking Techniques, Uchi Waza

A strike is an attack with a part of the human body intended to cause an effect or to simply cause harm to an opponent. There are many different varieties of strikes. An attack with the hand closed into a fist is called a punch, an attack with the leg or foot is referred to as a kick, and an attack with the head is called a head butt. There are also other differences in use in the martial arts.

The Japanese martial artist makes a distinction between punching and striking, which might not make sense to you at this time. The difference is like that of stabbing and slashing in the case of a sword. The striking is usually accomplished by a snapping motion from the elbow. The transmission of the force does not occur like a thrust on a straight line, but usually from a half circle, as you will see in the following pages. Many striking techniques can also be used in defense. Here is a short list of common striking techniques:

Back fist strike (uraken-Uchi or riken-Uchi)

Bottom fist strike (tettsui-uchi)

Backhand strike (haishu-uchi)

Knife-hand strike (shuto-uchi)

Ridge-hand strike (haito-uchi)

Palm heel strike (teisho-uchi)

Elbow strike (empi-uchi)

Hammer fist strike (tettsui-uchi)

Uraken Uchi (裏拳打) Back Fist Strike

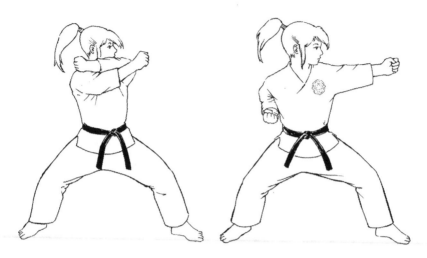

This technique includes the so-called uchi or indirect attack and is done with the back of the fist, particularly the area of the knuckles. At the moment of contact, the fist turns so that the small-finger side points down.

O'Sensei says that once you condition your hands, the back fist can cause a great deal of damage. It is used to attack the upper part of the body as well as the lower part of the body. When practicing with a partner, you must be very careful not to hurt your partner. Usually an attack is made to the face, temple area, solar plexus, side of the ribs, or back of the head. It is an all-around technique.

In the sideward strike, the back of the fist is used. The fist is propelled from the elbow, crossing the body from your right to your left, as seen in the illustration above. At the moment of contact, the fist turns so that the small-finger side points down.

Remember kime. The back of the fist must strike at the same moment as the leg is put down. Practice to the right as well as to the left. When I practice it, I usually use the horse stance position.

猿臂打ち **Empi-Uchi Elbow Strikes**

The elbow is one of the stronger karate weapons because of both the power that develops and the hardness of the used area. The age empi-uchi rising elbow strike is a very useful and powerful technique used in close-in fighting. It can be used in four separate techniques: forward strike, upward strike, sideward strike, and backward strike. It is used to strike the chin, face, ribs, and solar plexus.

All these techniques may be performed from the forward stance or the diagonal straddle-leg stance. All its variants need high accuracy, because a small displacement of the center of gravity or an attempt to give greater scope to the attack loses effectiveness. It is therefore necessary to concentrate force at the right time and help the opposite arm, which also acts as hikite, to grab and attract the opponent to the effective distance. Attacks are always accompanied by a shift from the hip in the same direction as the attacking arm. As there are many variants to the strike, the path of the elbow will determine the intended target.

Ushiro-Empi-Uchi – Back Elbow Strike

Ushiro-empi is a beautiful technique if properly executed. As you notice, the left arm is punching, while at the same time, the right arm is executing an elbow blow. Both arm techniques must be done at the same time. This technique is usually done in the horse stance.

Mae Empi-Uchi (猿臂打ち) Front Elbow Strike

Mae Empi-Uchi is delivered by placing the striking arm tightly against the hip with the palm of the fist facing up. The opposite arm is extended forward with the hand open as though attempting to grab and pull the opponent toward you. The strike is initiated by moving the striking arm forward in a semi-circular direction and at the same time pulling or withdrawing the opposite arm back toward the torso. The torso rotates at the same time and creates momentum and exaggerated power. As the striking arm moves forward impact should be with the forearm and elbow. It is important to keep in mind that the withdrawing arm must retract with at least as much speed and force as the striking arm in order to maximize the power of the strike.

Age Empi-Uchi—Upward Elbow Strike

The upward elbow strike brings the hardest part of your body – your elbow – up against your opponent's jaw from below. It can lift him off the ground, break his jaw, and even knock him out.

Otoshi Empi-Uchi

This is another effective variant of the empi-uchi strike. It consists of a downward strike of the elbow and is performed as is illustrated below. Speed of the withdrawing arm and rotation of the hips is important for proper execution of this strike.

Shuto-Uchi

This is an excellent striking technique in which a quick snap of the elbow and the twist of the wrist are used in attacking the opponent's neck with the edge of the hand. Bring your hand smoothly to your ear with the elbow bent. When executing shuto-uchi, swing wide in an arc to the target, as you see in the drawings. Strike with the edge of the hand below the little finger.

The shuto-uchi may be performed from zenkutsu-dachi (front stance) as well as from sochin-dachi (diagonal stance).

Here is another view of shuto-uchi from the front.

Haishu-Uchi Backhand Strike

This is simply a backhand strike also used as a block. It is used mainly against an attack to the solar plexus. The advantage of this technique is that after blocking, it is easy to grasp the opponent's arm and pull him off balance or follow up with a counterattack. It is an excellent technique.

Haito-Uchi Ridge-Hand Strike

This is a very delicate technique. One must use discretion when using this technique. The ridge hand is the edge of the hand on the thumb side, below the index finger.

You may strike with a wide arc, snapping the arm directly to your opponent's side of the neck. You may also strike the ridge of the nose if you are positioned to the side.

Tettsui-Uchi Hammer-Fist Strike

This is exactly the same as a riken-uchi except that the little-finger side of the fist is used in striking a hammer blow.

Nukite Spear Hand

Nukite is the sharp strike of the fingers extended into the soft body parts of your opponent. Use your fingers to strike the opponent. You can use all your fingers or just your first two. Make sure you keep your thumb tucked in. Unless you have strong fingers, I recommend you only use this technique to strike your opponent's soft spots. (The soft spots are the eyes, throat, temples, armpits, groin, etc.) A nukite strike has a slightly longer reach than a simple punch, so for that reason, you may wish to condition your fingers and get used to nukite strikes.

Chapter Thirteen: Blocking

There are many blocking techniques in karate—so many it is hard to list or explain them all. We will study the most common basic blocks. Blocking simply means using whatever you can to prevent your opponent from striking you. Since karate itself is a system without other weapons, blocks are performed using various body parts, such as hands, arms, legs, and feet. Is the block important? You bet it is! Without a good and effective block, your opponent will likely connect with you—and believe me, it does not feel good to be hit, no matter how slight the strike is. Also, a good block will set you up to do a counterstrike to your opponent. Here are some of the blocks I have learned and now use in my karate training:

1. Age uke (rising block)
2. Gedan barai (downward block)
3. Uchi ude uke (inside/outside forearm block)
4. Soto ude uke (outside/inside forearm block)
5. Morote uke (augmented block)
6. Shuto uke (knife hand block)
7. Osae uke (pressing block)
8. Heiko uke (wedge block)
9. Teisho uke (palm heel block)
10. Gaiwan kaki wake uke (wedge block)
11. Haishu uke (back hand block)
12. Juji uke or kosa uke (cross block)
13. Sukui uke (scooping block)
14. Yama uke (mountain block)
15. Tsuki uke (punching block)
16. Tekubi kake uke (hooking wrist block)
17. Chudan kake uke

O'Sensei makes me stand in the stances for a long time. He says that it will make my leg muscles very strong. I also practice my hip rotation while I step forward and backward up and down the floor. Then he teaches me how to move in different directions and to use different stances in different directions. I practice these basic blocks every day without fail.

I practice my hip rotation from the half front facing to the front facing over and over again. I also do stepping and hip rotation exercises. Hip rotation helps to focus all the tension of my muscles upon impact with the target. O'Sensei says that this concept is called *kime*. This word suggests that one will make techniques decisive and strong.

Note: For the sake of space, all techniques are usually performed from the ready position, open-leg stance (hachiji-dachi).

Age Uke (Rising Block)

The term *age uke,* which translates to "rising block" or "upward block," is frequently used interchangeably with *jōdan uke* (high-level block). Age uke may be used to easily block or deflect an incoming high attack. Alternately, it may be used to receive an incoming attack, sweeping it overhead while maintaining contact with the attacking instrument (limb or weapon).

Age uke is one of the first blocks you learn in karate. The nature of age uke is that it travels in an upward direction and is the perfect block against punches to the face or downward attacks to the head and face (for example, if someone were going to hit you on the head with a club).

The preparing hand begins to pull back to the hip (hikite), while the other arm begins to travel across to the center of the body, ready to travel upward. The returning arm draws closer to the hip, and the blocking arm travels further upward. Upon finishing the block, the blocking forearm rotates 180 degrees, as you see in the drawing above.

Gedan Baraii (Downward Block)

This is a great block in karate. The downward block is frequently found in the kata forms. Beginners learn gedan baraii in the first kata in traditional karate (heian shodan) It is practiced first with an open-leg stance (natural stance) and then is progressed to the different stances. It is an excellent block against kicking techniques.

Standing in hachiji-dachi (natural stance) in a yoi (ready) position, bend the left forearm up until the fist reaches near the right ear while the right arm moves slightly in to the middle. The left elbow should be resting in the elbow pit of the right arm. Fling the left arm straight in front of you while pulling back the right fist to the right hip (hikite).

During this movement, your hips should swiftly rotate clockwise to add power. The rotation of the hips must be swift and stop the instant the fists stop at the final position. Another simultaneous event is the retracting hand landing on the hip; and last and most important of all, a sharp exhalation must be done through the nose, with an extremely abrupt stop at the moment the fist lands. The amount of hip rotation should be about thirty degrees (from the direction feet are pointing, i.e., straight forward = 0°), with the feet static, firmly gripping on the ground. This finishes a gedan baraii executed with the left arm. To do it with the right arm, simply mirror the actions.

Uchi Ude Uke (Inside/Outside Forearm Block)

Ude uke is a technique favored by many karate athletes. This is a strong defensive technique and is used to block an attack to the chest and to the face. There are two types of forearm blocks: the inside block and the outside block.

Let us study the inside block. It is called uchi ude uke. It is a very strong technique. The blocking surface is the forearm on the thumb side very close to the wrist. To help generate both speed and power with the block, always keep your arms and body connected. Do not let the arms drift away and thereby lose connection. As your blocking arm moves forward, your opposite arm will naturally pull back in the "opposite" direction. The blocking arm "twists" or rotates as it completes its motion. The opposite hand is now positioned for a strike.

Soto Ude Uke (Outside/Inside Forearm Block)

Moving the right leg forward from one stance to the next, raise the right arm up to the side, as shown, with the left hand forward (palm down) and hips around to the front of the body, pulling the left fist back to the hip and turning the hips and body sideways. Remember to apply the hamni principle that we discussed earlier.

Morote Uke (Augmented Block)

Morote uke can be used against an arm or leg attack. Although this is a two-handed block, one hand does the blocking, and the other strengthens and supports the block.

Begin with both arms down. Take a step forward either in fudo-dachi or zenkutsu-dachi. At the same time, begin with both hands down. At the same time, pull both hands up and quickly block, as you see me doing in the drawings. Block with the left arm in an inside/outside forearm block, with the right arm following at the same time, using the right fist next to the blocking elbow, where it will support the action. This is a very powerful block. It should be practiced diligently.

Shuto Uke (Knife Hand Block)

The Japanese word *shutô* means "hand sword technique." Shuto uke in kokutsu-dachi or knife hand block in back stance is probably one of the most awkward karate techniques in traditional karate, but it is the most beautiful once you have mastered the techniques.

The blocking arm position for a hand block is approximately a fist to a fist and a half distance from the body. There should be a ninety-degree bend at the blocking arm's elbow. The fingertips of the blocking hand are approximately shoulder height, with the shoulders down and relaxed. The blocking hand should be at a slight angle, so do not have the palm facing completely down or the edge of the hand blade facing down. The hand blade is somewhere in between. A good measure is having the back of the bent thumb on the blocking shuto facing directly at you at completion of the block.

The hikite (pulling arm) is placed right beneath the breasts so that the edge of the hand is on the solar plexus, fingertips approximately in line with the forward side of the body. Fingers and wrist should be straight, at the same time keeping the thumb bent and tight. Feel like you are pulling the tip of the thumb to the base of the thumb, on the inside of the hand. The whole length of the hikite arm, from elbow to fingertips, should be parallel with the floor.

So now you have the arm positions for shuto uke. You must keep practicing the finished arm positions. Feel the arm muscle working when you kime or tighten the muscles. Practice this on both sides. *Good luck!*

Osae Uke (Pressing Block)

This is similar to the sweeping block, except that the opponent's arm is pressed down and the counterattack delivered simultaneously. This technique is used mainly for blocking an attack to the abdomen or lower area.

Heiko Uke (Wedge Block)

A double block refers to either the simultaneous use of two separate blocks or executing one block that changes into another. When carefully used, double blocks can be extremely effective against an attack.

This is a double-handed block in which the inner surface of the wrist is used to block a double-fist punch. The wedge block may be executed with basically any stance in karate. However, when executed in the katas, usually it is performed in the zenkutsu-dachi or fudo-dachi stances. Cross both wrists in front of the chest, fists at shoulder level, palms facing inward. Move both arms forward to separate the attacker's hands, preventing him or her from using both hands to grab your neck. Cross your arms and quickly open your arms; your fists should be shoulder high.

Twist your forearms outward and your arms apart at the moment of impact. Twist your wrist strongly to add power to the block. Move your forward guarding arm behind you at the same time that you twist your other wrist and elbow forward. This will also add power to the block.

Teisho Uke (Palm Heel Block)

This is an exciting technique using the palm of your hand to block and strike. In the palm heel block, you're going to use the heel, as they say, of your palm. Tuck your fingers nice and tight when you block. This technique may also be used to strike your opponent. The palm heel is a very strong technique.

Once you have blocked with your palm heel, you can always use your fingers to rake back, sort of like a tiger-claw technique . You can use it as a strike, and also use it as a grab. Once you grab, you can finish up with another technique. Keep in mind that when you're actually hitting somebody, you can cause a lot of damage.

Gaiwan Kaki Wake Uke (Wedge Block)

This technique is similar to heiko uke, also called the wedge block. This is a double-handed block in which the outer surface of the wrist is used to block a double-fist punch. It also can be used to defend against an opponent who is trying to choke you. It can be used for someone attempting to grab your lapel.

With this block, you can also grasp the arms, thereby controlling your opponent. You may apply a knee kick or a close-quarters technique like an elbow to the face.

Haishu Uke (Back Hand Block)

The back hand block (haishu uke) is used to protect the middle body section as well as the upper body section. In the front stance, the arms are crossed in front of the body, with the blocking arm underneath the other arm, as you see in the drawing. The hand is open and the palm downward. With the palm still downward, the blocking hand moves outward using the action of the shoulders and elbow. In the final stage of the technique, outward rotation of the forearm brings the blocking surface to face outside and the palm toward the center of the body. The forearm rotation is about ninety degrees. You may also practice this technique in the horse stance.

Juji Uke (X Block)

This technique is usually performed from stances that are very strong to the front, that is, the front stance and the diagonal stance. To ensure that the block will be effective, every effort should be made to block a kicking attack in its initial stages. Therefore, special attention should be paid to timing.

Advanced Blocking Techniques

There are a number of blocks that appear in the more advanced katas. They are generally used in very specific situations and therefore, not practiced until one has mastered the more basic blocking techniques. We will briefly discuss a few of these techniques so that you have an awareness of them and their potential use.

Sukui Uke (Scooping Block)

The scooping block is a beautiful technique. There are several scooping blocks in traditional karate. They are used to catch slow kicks. The standard shown here is the open-hand scoop. This technique consists of scooping the opponent's attacking leg with a strong arc, the arm making a strong semicircle, and blocking with the forearm to strongly break the opponent's balance.

Yama Uke (Mountain Block)

This is a beautiful technique. It uses both forearms at the same time to block an attack to the face. It may be used on either side. This technique is used in the Shotokan kata Jutte.

Tsuki Uke (Punching Block)

This is actually a punching attack and a block performed in one movement. With the arm slightly curved to ward off an opponent's attack with the outside surface of the arm, a fore-fist straight punch is simultaneously delivered to the face.

Tebuki Kake Uke (Hooking Wrist Block)

This technique involves rotating the forearm outward while hooking and pressing the opponent's arm. It is especially suitable when a punch is directed to your stomach. Learning the hooking wrist block begins with practice in the open-leg stance. The blocking arm is palm downward, fingers of the blocking hand extended. In a semicircular motion, the blocking hand is brought up to shoulder level and then into the final position. This action comes from bending the wrist and the 180-degree outward rotation of the forearm, bringing the palm upward.

Chapter Fourteen: Kicking Techniques

In traditional karate, the feet as well as the hands are important weapons. Even if we do not have special training, O'Sensei explains that usually we use our hands to defend and attack. He says that one must practice the kicks more, to try to educate the legs for kicking. It is very important to limber up our legs through stretching and body exercises, since the whole body is used to execute a kick.

There are two types of kicking techniques: snap kick and thrust kick. The snap kick is more like a jabbing strike and, although useful, not as powerful as a thrust kicks. As you snap your kick and make contact with the target, you quickly pull the leg back. In the thrust kick, you fully extend the kicking leg and strike the target with such force you move it away from its original position. O'Sensei says that a good kick requires good strong balance, especially for the supporting leg. Remember that the supporting leg usually shifts and holds up your body weight. Therefore, it requires a strong, well-balanced stance.

Be ready to work out and practice as hard as you can. Develop your kicks; however, remember to warm up before you start kicking. When practicing kicks, be aware of your surroundings so you do not hit a wall or your karate companions. Here are some of the basic and most useful kicks.

Have fun!

Mae Geri (Front Kick)

This kick uses a snapping action from the knee, with the ball of the foot as your striking surface.

From either a zenkutsu-dachi (front stance) or fudo-dachi (rooting stance), the knee of the rear leg is quickly raised forward to a point in front of your chest. With the knee high in front of the chest, start to thrust your hips forward, while at the same time extending the ball of your foot (koshi) toward the target. Then thrust your hips forward and snap your leg straight, striking into the target.

After striking the target, the foot snaps back to a defensive posture in front of your body, prepared to strike again or drive forward with a hand technique using your upraised knee as protection. As O'Sensei has said many times, "The foot needs to come back faster than it goes out."

Mae Geri Kekomi (Front Thrusting Kick)

This kick is basically the same as mae geri (front kick), with the exception that you trust your hips forward to the target. The kekomi kick is a very strong technique when done properly.

Vincent A. Cruz

Yoko Geri Keage (Side Snapping Kick)

Standing in the straddle-leg stance, move the left leg in front of and beside the right leg. Pull the right knee upward to the side from behind the left leg, and while rotating the right hip upward, snap upward with the right foot. Rotate the hips back to their original position while snapping the right foot back to the left knee.

Yoko Geri Kekomi (Thrusting Side Kick)

This kick is similar to the yoko geri keage except that the leg is thrust out to the target. It is also a very strong technique.

Ushiro Geri (Back Kick)

With the left leg forward in the front stance, pull the back leg up toward the left leg, turning the body in a clockwise direction at that point. From here, snap the right leg up and thrust it back while looking over the right shoulder. Pull the right leg back to the left knee, and continue to turn the body in a clockwise direction.

Mawashi Geri (Roundhouse Kick)

Standing in front stance with the left leg forward, raise the right leg up to the side so that the knee is higher than the foot, with the right hip higher than the left. From this position, rotate the hips in a counterclockwise direction as the leg snaps around to the front. Pull the hips back to their original position, snapping the leg back at the same time. Move forward or backward into the front stance.

Nami Ashi (Inside Snapping Block)

The next couple of kicking techniques are blocking techniques.

The first one is nami ashi (shown above). It is a defensive technique against an attack to the groin and also to escape a stamping attack to the leg. It is a very speedy defense.

This technique is practiced from the straddle-leg stance. Since it is performed very quickly, the body weight is not shifted. As you practice, you will notice that the hip movement has a lot to do with snapping the leg upward. Only the blocking leg moves, leaving the rest of the body free to prepare for the next technique.

You can also perform this technique from the straddle-leg stance (kiba-dachi), diagonal straddle-leg stance (sochin-dachi), and forward stance (zenkutsu-dachi).

Mikazuki Geri (Crescent Kick)

This is called the crescent kick. From the horse stance, swing the leg and hook the foot in the direction of your opponent, striking the upper portion of his or her body. This kick is also frequently used as a foot blocking technique, using the sole of your foot as the striking surface in a wide circular motion. Make sure you are balanced when performing the block. This technique may be performed to the side as well as to the front.

Mae Tobi Geri (Flying Front Kick)

In karate, we sometimes jump in the air and execute kicking techniques. These techniques require a lot of practice. There are many variations, and it is very exciting to do them. The most basic one is the flying front kick. This kick is a surprise attack to the stomach chin, and face.

Starting from a forward stance, jump and snap to the front with the left leg, as you see me doing. Simultaneously jump up and forward with the right leg, snapping a front kick. You must withdraw the left leg at the same time you kick with the right leg. At this time, your body should be at its highest point. Withdraw the right leg very quickly and land in your original stance. Remember: it take a lot of practice and agility to do the flying front kick.

Yoko Tobi Geri (Flying Side Kick)

Like the flying front kick, this technique is most commonly used as a surprise attack. It may be used to dodge an opponent's attack, as a counterattack to the side of his or her neck or head.

From the front stance, jump up with the left leg, simultaneously bringing the right knee close to your chest. While pulling your leg close to your body, side thrust and kick with the left leg. When the kick is completed, withdraw the kicking leg and return to the original forward stance.

Fumi-Komi (Stomping Kick)

This is a downward-directed kick, which you can use forward, sideward, or backward against the shin. It can also be used to the bridge of the foot or the back of the knee. It is also used against an opponent who is on the ground, attacking the head or stomach.

The below illustration shows the stomping kick in action.

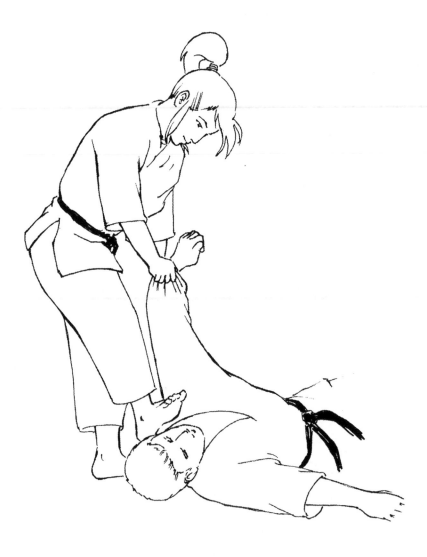

Chapter Fifteen: The Kata

O'Sensei explains that the kata is one of a number of preset defenses and attacks conducted in a fixed sequence to demonstrate methods of defense, attack, and counterattack. O'Sensei says that there are about fifty ancient katas. It was not until about fifty years ago that the kata was considered the ideal form of karate. Master Gichin Funakoshi, the founder of modern karate, revised these ancient katas. Of these, he chose twenty-five katas, which are still being practiced today in the traditional karate system.

The positions, movements, and individual techniques must be mastered in strength and precision. O'Sensei says that for this reason, kata is considered an excellent basic training for the development of good karate techniques—balance, self-assured movements, forceful attacks, and precise defense. With discipline and practice, your karate will improve. I have included a very basic kata to give you an idea what it looks like. If you are a beginner, it will give you a basic kata to practice.

On the next page, I introduce the first kata of the Shotokan system. This kata is called heian shodan, which means "peace of mind, first step." It is considered the easiest kata in the system. The next drawing shows all of the steps of this kata. The shape formed by the series of movements is called the "embusen." Next, I will move through the kata step-by-step and describe each movement from start to finish. Notice how I end my kata with a kiai, and after a two- second pause, I move back to the ready position and should be in the same spot I started from.

Vincent A. Cruz

Kata Heian Shodan

Heian Shodan

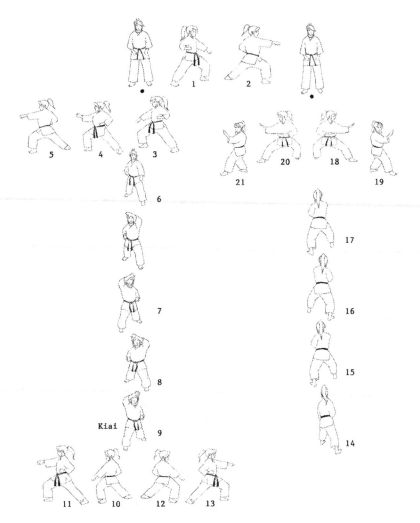

120

Movements

- Ready Position
1. Look to the left and execute a downward block.
2. Continue forward and execute a forward punch.

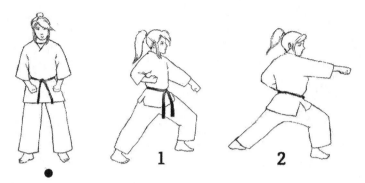

3. Turning 180 degrees to the right, execute a right downward block.
4. Bring your right foot back about one third and quickly step forward; at the same time, execute a downward hammer fist.
5. Quickly take a step forward with the left foot and execute a left forward punch.

6. Turn left and execute a downward block in front stance.

Raise your left arm slowly to an upward block; however, the hand is open.

7. Come forward and execute an upward block.

8. Continue forward and execute another upward block.

9. Continue forward and execute another (extra strong) upward block and kiai.

Kiai

10. Spin 270 degrees to the left and execute a left downward block.
11. Continue forward and execute a right forward punch.
12. Turn 180 degrees to the right and execute a right downward block.
13. Continue and execute a strong left forward punch.

11   **10**   **12**   **13**

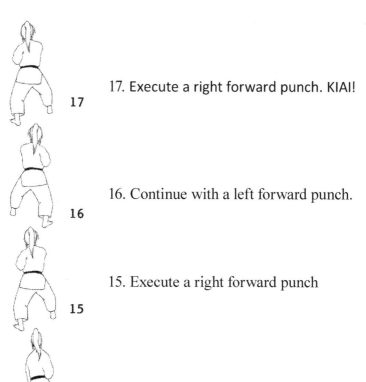

17. Execute a right forward punch. KIAI!

16. Continue with a left forward punch.

15. Execute a right forward punch

14. Turn to the left and execute a strong downward block.

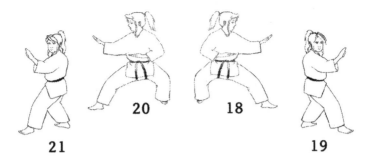

18. Turn 270 degrees to the left and execute a back stance; at the same time, execute a left knife hand block.

19. Step to 45 degrees and execute a right knife hand block.

20. Turn clockwise 135 degrees and execute a left knife hand block.

21. Step to the left and execute a left knife hand block at 45-degrees.

Back to the ready position and the kata is finished.

Chapter Sixteen: Combining Techniques

O'Sensei tells us that techniques are not isolated and are the direct result of some other action. They can also be used together to form "combinations," which might include blocks, punches, strikes, and kicks—in any combination! Combining techniques takes time and is the end product of many hours of practice and study. As Shotokan is a system of karate, each technique is built from other techniques that have already been learned. To be able to perform a new technique properly, you must first master the prior technique. With practice and careful study, this becomes natural and almost automatic.

Position of the Body

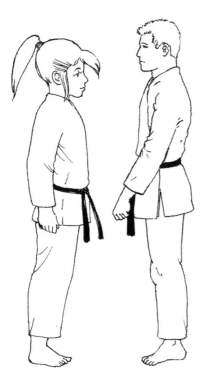

Karate is the mastery of balance. With little exception, the body and spine must always remain straight. At times you may turn your body sideways in order to present fewer targets to your opponent. You turn your body to the side mainly for defense, however, to transform the power of instantly counterturning and counterattack.

When practicing the following combinations, you must begin each instance at the ready position. Self-defense always begins at the ready position. Remember: while you stand, you must have a stable feeling of your emotions. You must relax your body, although you are mentally prepared and aware of your surroundings. Also remember, practice makes perfect. I usually practice with my brother, Roberto Marcus.

Downward Block/Reverse Punch

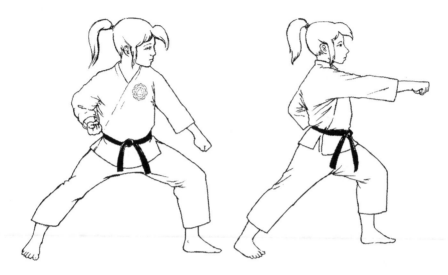

1. Stand in the ready position.
2. As your opponent attacks you, immediately step back and execute a downward block.
3. Follow up with a reverse punch to the chest. Kiai.
4. Quickly step back to the ready position.

Upward Block/Reverse Punch

1. Stand in the ready position.
2. As your opponent attacks you, immediately step back and execute an upward block.
3. Quickly execute a reverse punch to the head (kiai).
4. Quickly step back to the ready position.

Forearm Block/Reverse Punch

1. Stand in the ready position.
2. As your opponent attacks you to your chest, immediately step back and execute a forearm block.
3. Follow up with a forward punch to the chest. Kiai.
4. Quickly step back to the ready position.

Forearm Block / Uraken Uchi

1. Your opponent attacks with a front punch.
2. Step back into side stance and deflect a punch with an outside forearm block.
3. Attack his ribs or solar plexus with a backfist (uraken uchi) or hammerfist (tettsui uchi) strike.

Downward Block/Roundhouse Kick

1. From the ready position, quickly execute a downward block.
2. Quickly follow up with a roundhouse kick to the face.
3. Remember to focus and kiai.

Downward Block / Front Thrusting Kick

1. From the ready position, execute a downward block in the front stance.
2. Quickly follow up with a strong front thrust kick (kiai).

Downward Block /Front Snapping Kick/Reverse Punch

1. Stand in the ready position.
2. As your opponent attacks you, immediately execute a downward block.
3. Quickly execute a front kick to the chest or to the head (kiai).
4. Follow up with a reverse punch to the chest.
5. Quickly step back to the ready position.

Osae-Uke Pressing Block/Reverse Punch

1. Stand in the ready position.
2. As your opponent attacks your middle line, take a step back in back stance, and immediately execute a pressing block.
3. Quickly execute a reverse punch to your opponent (kiai).
4. Quickly step back to the ready position.

Back-of-Hand Block/Reverse Punch

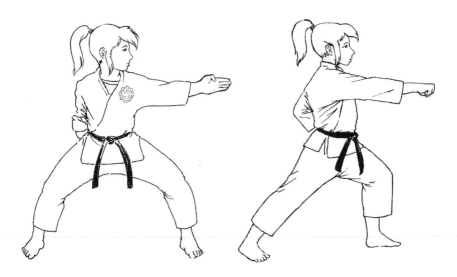

1. Stand in a ready posture.
2. Once the attacker attacks your face, quickly step back to a horse stance and at the same time block with a left back-of-the-hand block.
3. Quickly grasp his hand and execute a reverse punch. Kiai!

Palm Heel Block / Palm heel strike

1. In the ready position step backward in the front stance and execute a palm heel block.
2. In the palm heel block, you're going to use the heel, as they say, of your palm. Tuck your fingers nice and tight when you block. This technique may also be used to strike your opponent. The palm heel is a very strong technique.
3. Once you have blocked with your palm heel, you can always use your fingers to rake back, sort of like a tiger-claw technique . You can use it as a strike, and also use it as a grab. Once you grab, you can finish up with a palm heel strike to the face.

Mikazuki Geri (Crescent Kick Body Check)

1. If your opponent attacks with a forward punch, you can use a crescent kick to the chest to knock him out of stance and disrupt his attack.
2. Follow up with any technique you wish.

Mikazuki Geri Uke (Crescent Kick Block)

1. Your opponent attacks with a front punch.
2. Step back and quickly knock his punch aside with a crescent kick.
3. To counterattack, use a side-thrust kick or back kick from the same foot without setting it down first.

Kakuto Uke (Bent-Wrist Block)

1. Stand in the ready position.
2. You opponent attacks to the face. Step back and strike his arm from below with your bent wrist.
3. Retaliate with a strong reverse punch.

Morote Uke (Augmented Block)

1. Your opponent attacks with a front punch.
2. Step back and block with an augmented block.
3. Use a powerful reverse-punch to counter.

Nami Ashi (Inside Snapping Block)

1. If your opponent attacks you with a front kick, you might be able to ward him off with a nami ashi to throw him off balance.
2. Quickly attack your opponent with any frontal attack you wish.

Mawashi Tsuki Kihon Roundhouse Punch

1. This punch starts off as a straight punch; however, as the intended target is usually the side of the head, the path of the hand and arm includes a slight "hook."
2. The hooking motion, combined with a twist of the forearm, allows the fist to turn from a direct path to a slightly angled path and make contact as intended. The hooking motion gives the punch it's "roundhouse" name.

Glossary

age-uke	rising block
age zuki	rising punch or high punch
ashi-barai	foot sweep
bunkai	application (of kata moves)
choku-zuki	straight punch
chudan	middle-level defense
do-gi	training suit (for karate/judo/etc.)
dojo	training hall
empi-uchi	elbow strike
fudo-dachi	rooted stance
fumikomi-geri	stamping kick
gedan	defense lower level
gedan-barai	lower block/sweep
gyaku-hanme	half front facing to the opposite side
gyaku-zuki	reverse punch
hachiji-dachi	basic stance
haito-uchi	ridge-hand strike

hajime	start
hangetsu-dachi	half moon stance
hanme	half front facing
hara-	stomach
heisoku-dachi	feet together
hiza-geri	knee strike
ippom kumite-	one-step contest exercise
jiyu ippon kumite-	semifree sparring
jiyu kumite	freestyle contest
jodan-	upper-level defense
juji uke-	downward or upward X block
kage zuki:	hook punch
kamae	guard/posture
karate-gi	karate suit
karateka	karate practitioner
kata	prearranged forms
kiai	battle cry
kiba-dachi	horse/straddle stance
kihon	basics
kokutsu-dachi	back stance
kumite	sparring contest exercise

mae geri	front kick
mae tobi geri	foot attack from the air
mawashi geri	roundhouse kick
mawashi zuki	roundhouse punch
mawatte	turn
mokuso	meditation
morote uke	augmented block
morote zuki	punch with both fists
nagashi uke	sweeping block
naotte	relax/recover
neko-ashi-dachi	cat-foot stance
osae-uke	pressing block
O'Sensei	master instructor
otagai ni rei	bow to each other
otoshi uke	dropping block
oui zuki	lunge punch
sanbon kumite	three-step sparring exercise
sanchin-dachi	hourglass stance
seiken choku zuki	front punch or fist

seiza	formal kneeling position
sensei	instructor
sensei ni rei	bow to the instructor
shiko-dachi	squat/sumo stance
shizen-tai	natural stance
shomen	front facing
shomen ni rei	bow to the front
shuto uchi	blow with the edge of the hand
shuto-uke	knife hand block
sochin-dachi	rooted stance
soto ude uke	outer edge of forearm block
soto-uke	outside block
sukui uke	scooping block
tate zuki	punch with quarter-turn fist
tettsui uchi	hammer-fist strike
tobi-geri	jumping kick
uchi-(ude-)uke	inside (forearm) block
uraken-uchi	backfist strike
ura-mawashi-geri	reverse roundhouse kick
ura-zuki	upper cut

ushiro-geri	back kick
yame	stop
yoi	ready
yoko-geri-keage	side snap kick
yoko-geri-kekomi	side thrust kick
yoko tobi geri	side kick jump
zenkutsu-dachi	front stance

Suggested Reading List

- *Dynamic Karate* by Masatoshi Nakayama. Detailed explanations and photographs of all fundamental Shotokan techniques and how to apply them. Does not cover kata.
- *Karate: The Art of Empty-Hand Fighting* by Hidetaka Nishiyama. First published in 1960, this is one of the first books written in English on Shotokan. Provides detailed explanations and photographs of all the fundamental techniques. Also covers kumite and kata (but only heian yondan).
- *Best Karate, Vol.1: Comprehensive* by Masotoshi Nakayama. Demonstrates and explains the basic techniques, kumite and kata, of Shotokan.
- *Shotokan Karate: A Precise History* by Harry Cook. Covers the history of Shotokan from Okinawa to Japan and its subsequent dissemination internationally.

About the Author

Vincent A. Cruz is an experienced martial artist and an advocate of traditional karate. He is the founder and chief instructor of the International San Ten Karate Association (ISKA) and the International San Ten Martial Arts Federation (ISTMAF), where he holds the rank of tenth-degree black belt. "San Ten" refers to Cruz's "three heavens" (physical, mental, and spiritual) philosophy of karate. ISKA is dedicated to the facilitation of harmonious relations, mutual respect, brotherhood, and the acceptance of all traditions of martial artistry, regardless of style or system practiced.

Cruz was born in Brooklyn, New York, in 1937, the son of immigrant parents of Puerto Rican and Italian descent. Following graduation from high school in 1954, Cruz immediately joined the United States Air Force and was stationed at Ashiya in southern Japan. He began karate training in March 1956 under Kaigate O. (a student of Kyan Chotoky). Later, in 1956, the Air Force transferred Cruz to Tokyo, where Isao Obata introduced him to Shotokan karate training.

In June 1959, he was selected as an instructor for the Strategic Air Command (SAC) Combative Measure Program held at the Kodokan Judo Institute. During this time, Cruz was instructed in a comprehensive program by Masters Kyuzo Mifune and H. Kotani in judo; Masters Isao Obata and Hidetaka Nishiyama in karate-do; Master T. Tomiki in aikido; and Master M. Hosakawa in taijo-jutsu. During this period, Cruz attained a shodan in judo, certification in taijo-jutsu and aikido, as well as a shodan in Shotokan karate. Upon returning to the United States, Cruz continued his karate training under Hidetaka Nishiyama.

Today, Cruz is a sixth-degree black belt in the AAKF and ITKA and a tenth-degree black belt in ISKA and ISTMAF. He also holds a sixth-degree black belt in the Nippon Karate Do Kyo Kai. He is a certified martial arts instructor and examiner under the AAKF and the ITKF; both headed by the late Hidetaka Nishiyama. He is usually addressed with the honorific title "Hanshi" and has authored or coauthored two books regarding traditional karate. With fifty-five years of karate training, Master Cruz has been providing karate instruction at all levels for nearly fifty years.

Cruz received his Bachelor of Arts degree from Southern Illinois University, Carbondale, in 1984. On May 10, 2002, Representative George Radanovich ordered a US flag flown over the Capitol Building in Washington DC in honor of Cruz's distinguished military career and lifelong contributions. He has four children, thirteen grandchildren, and three great grandchildren who live on the West Coast, where he is located and spends most of his time. Today, Cruz travels the United States and internationally giving seminars and promoting the teaching and philosophical elements of traditional karate.